WINTER JOURNAL

Paul Auster is the bestselling author of *Invisible*, *Man in the Dark*, *The Brooklyn Follies*, *The Book of Illusions*, and *The New York Trilogy*, among many other works. In 2006 he was awarded the Prince of Asturias Prize for Literature and inducted into the American Academy of Arts and Letters. Among his other honours are the Independent Spirit Award for the screenplay of *Smoke* and the Prix Médicis étranger for *Leviathan*. He has also been shortlisted for both the International IMPAC Dublin Literary Award (*The Book of Illusions*) and the PEN/Faulkner Award for Fiction (*The Music of Chance*). His work has been translated into more than thirty languages. He lives in Brooklyn, New York.

also by Paul Auster

FICTION

The New York Trilogy
In the Country of Last Things
Moon Palace
The Music of Chance
Leviathan
Mr Vertigo
Timbuktu
The Book of Illusions
Oracle Night
The Brooklyn Follies
Travels in the Scriptorium
Man in the Dark
Invisible
Sunset Park
Collected Novels: Volume One
Collected Novels: Volume Two
Collected Novels: Volume Three

NON-FICTION

The Invention of Solitude
The Art of Hunger
Hand to Mouth
Collected Prose

SCREENPLAYS

Smoke & Blue in the Face
Lulu on the Bridge
The Inner Life of Martin Frost
Collected Screenplays

POETRY

Collected Poems

EDITOR

True Tales of American Life

TRANSLATION

Chronicle of the Guayaki Indians
by Pierre Clastres

WINTER JOURNAL

PAUL AUSTER

ff
faber and faber

First published in the USA in 2012
by Henry Holt and Company, LLC
175 Fifth Avenue
New York, New York 10010

First published in the UK in 2012
by Faber and Faber Ltd
Bloomsbury House
74–77 Great Russell Street
London WC1B 3DA
This export paperback edition first published in 2012

Printed and bound in the UK by CPI Group (UK) Ltd, Croydon CR0 4YY

A CIP record for this book
is available from the British Library

ISBN 978–0–571–28321–7

2 4 6 8 10 9 7 5 3 1

WINTER JOURNAL

You think it will never happen to you, that it cannot happen to you, that you are the only person in the world to whom none of these things will ever happen, and then, one by one, they all begin to happen to you, in the same way they happen to everyone else.

Your bare feet on the cold floor as you climb out of bed and walk to the window. You are six years old. Outside, snow is falling, and the branches of the trees in the backyard are turning white.

Speak now before it is too late, and then hope to go on speaking until there is nothing more to be said. Time is running out, after all. Perhaps it is just as well to put aside your stories for now and try to examine what it has felt like to live inside this body from the first day you can remember being alive until this one. A catalogue of sensory data. What one might call a *phenomenology of breathing.*

You are ten years old, and the midsummer air is warm, oppressively warm, so humid and uncomfortable that even as you sit in the shade of the trees in the backyard, sweat is gathering on your forehead.

It is an incontestable fact that you are no longer young. One month from today, you will be turning sixty-four, and although that is not excessively old, not what anyone would consider to be an advanced old age, you cannot stop yourself from thinking about all the others who never managed to get as far as you have. This is one example of the various things that could never happen, but which, in fact, have happened.

The wind in your face during last week's blizzard. The awful sting of the cold, and you out there in the empty streets wondering what possessed you to leave the house in such a pounding storm, and yet, even as you struggled to keep your balance, there was the exhilaration of that wind, the joy of seeing the familiar streets turned into a blur of white, whirling snow.

Physical pleasures and physical pains. Sexual pleasures first and foremost, but also the pleasures of food and drink, of lying naked in a hot bath, of scratching an itch, of sneezing and farting, of spending an extra hour in bed, of turning your face toward the sun on a mild afternoon in late spring or early summer and feeling the warmth settle upon your skin. Innumerable instances, not a day gone by without some moment or moments of physical pleasure, and yet pains are no doubt more persistent and intractable, and at one time or another nearly every part of your body has been subjected to assault.

Eyes and ears, head and neck, shoulders and back, arms and legs, throat and stomach, ankles and feet, not to mention the enormous boil that once sprouted on the left cheek of your ass, referred to by the doctor as a *wen*, which to your ears sounded like some medieval affliction and prevented you from sitting in chairs for a week.

The proximity of your small body to the ground, the body that belonged to you when you were three and four years old, that is to say, the shortness of the distance between your feet and head, and how the things you no longer notice were once a constant presence and preoccupation for you: the little world of crawling ants and lost coins, of fallen twigs and dented bottle caps, of dandelions and clover. But especially the ants. They are what you remember best. Armies of ants traveling in and out of their powdery hills.

You are five years old, crouched over an anthill in the backyard, attentively studying the comings and goings of your tiny six-legged friends. Unseen and unheard, your three-year-old neighbor creeps up behind you and strikes you on the head with a toy rake. The prongs pierce your scalp, blood flows into your hair and down the back of your neck, and you run screaming into the house, where your grandmother tends to your wounds.

Your grandmother's words to your mother: "Your father would be such a wonderful man—if only he were different."

This morning, waking in the dimness of another January dawn, a scumbled, grayish light seeping into the bedroom, and there is your wife's face turned toward your face, her eyes closed, still fast asleep, the covers pulled all the way up to her neck, her head the only part of her that is visible, and you marvel at how beautiful she looks, how young she looks, even now, thirty years after you first slept with her, after thirty years of living together under the same roof and sharing the same bed.

More snow falling today, and as you climb out of bed and walk to the window, the branches of the trees in the back garden are turning white. You are sixty-three years old. It occurs to you that there has rarely been a moment during the long journey from boyhood to now when you have not been in love. Thirty years of marriage, yes, but in the thirty years before that, how many infatuations and crushes, how many ardors and pursuits, how many deliriums and mad surges of desire? From the very start of your conscious life, you have been a willing slave of Eros. The girls you loved as a boy, the women you loved as a man, each one different from the others, some round and some lean, some short and some tall, some bookish and some athletic, some moody and some outgoing, some white and some black and some Asian, nothing on the surface ever mattered to you, it was all about the inner light you would detect in her, the spark of singularity, the blaze of revealed selfhood, and that light would make her beautiful to you, even if others were blind to the beauty you saw, and then you would burn to be with her, to be near her, for feminine beauty is something you have never been able to resist. All the way back to your first days of school, the kindergarten class in which you fell for the girl with the long blonde ponytail, and how often were you punished by Miss Sandquist for sneaking off with the little girl you had fallen for, the two of you together in a corner somewhere making mischief, but those punishments meant nothing to you, for you were in love, and you were a fool for love then, just as you are a fool for love now.

The inventory of your scars, in particular the ones on your face, which are visible to you each morning when you look into the bathroom mirror to shave or comb your hair. You seldom think about them, but whenever you do, you understand that they are marks of life, that the assorted jagged lines etched into the skin of your face are letters from the secret alphabet that tells the story of who you are, for each scar is the trace of a healed wound, and each wound was caused by an unexpected collision with the world—that is to say, an accident, or something that need not have happened, since by definition an accident is something that need not happen. Contingent facts as opposed to necessary facts, and the realization as you look into the mirror this morning that all life is contingent, except for the one necessary fact that sooner or later it will come to an end.

You are three and a half, and your twenty-five-year-old pregnant mother has taken you along with her on a shopping expedition to a department store in downtown Newark. She is accompanied by a friend of hers, the mother of a boy who is three and a half as well. At some point, you and your little comrade break away from your mothers and begin running through the store. It is an enormous open space, no doubt the largest room you have ever set foot in, and there is a palpable thrill in being able to run wild through this gargantuan indoor arena. Eventually, you and the boy begin belly-flopping onto the floor and sliding along the smooth surface, sledding without sleds, as it were, and this game proves to be so enjoyable, so ecstatic in the pleasure it produces, that you become more and more reckless, more and more daring in what you are willing to attempt. You reach a part of the store where construction work or repair work is under way, and without bothering to take notice of what obstacles might lie ahead, you belly-flop onto the floor again and sail along the glasslike surface until you find yourself speeding straight toward a wooden carpenter's bench. With a small twist of your small body, you think you can avoid crashing into the leg of the table that is looming before you, but what you do not realize in the split second you have to shift course is that a nail is jutting from the leg, a long nail low enough to be at the level of your face, and before you can stop yourself, your left cheek is pierced by the nail as you go flying past it. Half your face is torn apart. Sixty years later, you have no memories of the accident. You remember the running and the belly-flopping, but nothing about the pain, nothing about the blood, and nothing about being rushed to the hospital or the doctor who sewed up your cheek. He did a brilliant job, your mother always said, and since the trauma of seeing her firstborn with half his face ripped off never left her, she said it often: something to do with a subtle double-stitching method that kept the damage to a minimum and prevented you from being disfigured for life. You could have lost your eye, she would say to you—or, even more dramatically, You could have been killed. No doubt she was right. The scar has grown fainter and fainter as the years have passed, but it is still there whenever you look for it, and you will carry that emblem of good fortune (eye intact! not dead!) until you go to your grave.

Split eyebrow scars, one left and one right, almost perfectly symmetrical, the first caused by running full tilt into a brick wall during a dodgeball game in grade school gym class (the massively swollen black eye you sported for days afterward, which reminded you of a photograph of boxer Gene Fullmer, who had been defeated in a championship bout by Sugar Ray Robinson around the same time) and the second caused in your early twenties when you drove in for a layup during an outdoor basketball game, were fouled from behind, and flew into the metal pole supporting the basket. Another scar on your chin, origin unknown. Most likely from an early childhood spill, a hard fall onto a sidewalk or a stone that split open your flesh and left its mark, which is still visible whenever you shave in the morning. No story accompanies this scar, your mother never talked about it (at least not that you can recall), and you find it odd, if not downright perplexing, that this permanent line was engraved on your chin by what can only be called *an invisible hand*, that your body is the site of events that have been expunged from history.

It is June 1959. You are twelve years old, and in one week you and your sixth-grade classmates will be graduating from the grammar school you have attended since you were five. It is a splendid day, late spring in its most lustrous incarnation, sunlight pouring down from a cloudless blue sky, warm but not too warm, scant humidity, a soft breeze stirring the air and rippling over your face and neck and bare arms. Once school lets out for the day, you and a gang of your friends repair to Grove Park for a game of pickup baseball. Grove Park is not a park so much as a kind of village green, a large rectangle of well-tended grass flanked by houses on all four sides, a pleasant spot, one of the loveliest public spaces in your small New Jersey town, and you and your friends often go there to play baseball after school, since baseball is the thing you all love most, and you play for hours on end without ever growing weary of it. No adults are present. You establish your own ground rules and settle disagreements among yourselves—most often with words, occasionally with fists. More than fifty years later, you remember nothing about the game that was played that afternoon, but what you do remember is the following: The game is over, and you are standing alone in the middle of the infield, playing catch with yourself, that is, throwing a ball high into the air and following its ascent and descent until it lands in your glove, at which point you immediately throw the ball into the air again, and each time you throw the ball it travels higher than it did the time before, and after several throws you are reaching unprecedented heights, the ball is hovering in the air for many seconds now, the white ball going up against the clear blue sky, the white ball coming down into your glove, and your entire being is engaged in this witless activity, your concentration is total, nothing exists now except the ball and the sky and your glove, which means that your face is turned upward, that you are looking up as you follow the trajectory of the ball, and therefore you are no longer aware of what is happening on the ground, and what happens on the ground as you are looking up at the sky is that something or someone unexpectedly comes crashing into you, and the impact is so sudden, so violent, so overwhelming in its force that you instantly fall to the ground, feeling as though you have been hit by a tank. The brunt of the blow was aimed at your head, in particular your forehead, but your torso has been battered as well, and as you lie on the ground gasping for breath, stunned and nearly unconscious, you see that blood is flowing from your forehead, no, not flowing, gushing, and so you remove your white T-shirt and press it against the gushing spot, and within seconds the white T-shirt has turned entirely red. The other boys are alarmed. They come rushing toward you to do what they can to help, and it is only then that you find out what happened. It seems that one of your cohort, a gangly, good-hearted lunkhead called B.T. (you remember his name but will not divulge it here, since you do not want to embarrass him—assuming he is still alive), was so impressed by your towering, skyscraper throws that he got it into *his head* to take part in the action, and without bothering to tell you that he, too, was going to try to catch one of your throws started running in the direction of the descending ball, head turned upward, of course, and mouth hanging open in that oafish way of his (what person runs with his mouth hanging open?), and when he crashed into you a moment later, running at an all-out gallop, the teeth protruding from his open mouth went straight into *your head*. Hence the blood now gushing out of you, hence the depth of the gash in the skin above your left eye. Fortunately, the office of your family doctor is just across the way, in one of the houses that line the perimeter of Grove Park. The boys decide to lead you there at once, and so you cross the park holding your bloody T-shirt against your head in the company of your friends, perhaps four of them, perhaps six of them, you no longer remember, and burst en masse into Dr. Kohn's office. (You have not forgotten his name, just as you have not forgotten the name of your kindergarten teacher, Miss Sandquist, or the names of any of the other teachers you had as a boy.) The receptionist tells you and your friends that Dr. Kohn is seeing a patient just now, and before she can get up from her chair to inform the doctor that there is an emergency to attend to, you and your friends march into the consulting room without bothering to knock. You find Dr. Kohn talking to a plump, middle-aged woman who is sitting on the examination table dressed in a bra and slip only. The woman lets out a yelp of surprise, but once Dr. Kohn sees the blood gushing from your forehead, he tells the woman to get dressed and leave, tells your friends to make themselves scarce, and then hastens to the task of sewing up your wound. It is a painful procedure, since there is no time to administer an anesthetic, but you do your best not to howl as he threads the stitches through your skin. The job he does is perhaps not as brilliant as the one executed by the doctor who sewed up your cheek in 1950, but it is effective for all that, since you do not bleed to death and no longer have a hole in your head. Some days later, you and your sixth-grade classmates take part in your grammar school graduation ceremony. You have been selected to be a flag-bearer, which means that you must carry the American flag down an aisle of the auditorium and plant it in the flag stand on stage. Your head is wrapped in a white gauze bandage, and because blood still seeps occasionally from the spot where you were stitched up, the white gauze has a large red stain on it. After the ceremony, your mother says that when you were walking down the aisle with the flag, you reminded her of a painting of a wounded Revolutionary War hero. You know, she says, just like *The Spirit of '76*.

What presses in on you, what has always pressed in on you: the outside, meaning the air—or, more precisely, your body in the air around you. The soles of your feet anchored to the ground, but all the rest of you exposed to the air, and that is where the story begins, in your body, and everything will end in the body as well. For now, you are thinking about the wind. Later, if time allows for it, you will think about the heat and the cold, the infinite varieties of rain, the fogs you have stumbled through like a man without eyes, the demented, machine-gun tattoo of hailstones clattering against the tile roof of the house in the Var. But it is the wind that claims your attention now, for the air is seldom still, and beyond the barely perceptible breath of nothingness that sometimes surrounds you, there are the breezes and wafting lilts, the sudden gusts and squalls, the three-day-long mistrals you lived through in that house with the tile roof, the soaking nor'easters that sweep along the Atlantic coast, the gales and hurricanes, the whirlwinds. And there you are, twenty-one years ago, walking through the streets of Amsterdam on your way to an event that has been canceled without your knowledge, dutifully trying to fulfill the commitment you have made, out in what will later be called *the storm of the century*, a hurricane of such blistering intensity that within an hour of your stubborn, ill-advised decision to venture outdoors, large trees will be uprooted in every corner of the city, chimneys will tumble to the ground, and parked cars will be lifted up and go sailing through the air. You walk with your face to the wind, trying to advance along the sidewalk, but in spite of your efforts to get to where you are going, you cannot move. The wind is blasting into you, and for the next minute and a half, you are stuck.

Your hands on the Ha'penny Bridge in Dublin thirteen Januarys ago, the night following another hurricane with hundred-mile-an-hour winds, the final night of the film you have been directing for the past two months, the last scene, the last shot, a simple matter of fixing the camera on the gloved hand of your leading actress as she turns her wrist and lets go of a small stone that will fall into the waters of the Liffey. There is nothing to it, no shot has demanded less effort or ingenuity in the entire film, but there you are in the dank and dark of the windswept night, as exhausted as you have ever been after nine weeks of grueling work on a production fraught with countless problems (budget problems, union problems, location problems, weather problems), fifteen pounds lighter than when you began, and after standing for hours on the bridge with your crew, the clammy, frigid Irish air has infiltrated your bones, and a moment comes just before the final shot when you realize that your hands are frozen, that you cannot move your fingers, that your hands have turned into two blocks of ice. Why aren't you wearing gloves? you ask yourself, but you are unable to answer the question, since the thought of gloves never even occurred to you when you left your hotel for the bridge. You film the last shot one more time, and then you and your producer, along with your actress, your actress's boyfriend, and several members of the crew, go to a nearby pub to thaw out and celebrate the completion of the film. The place is crowded, jammed full, an echo chamber packed with roaring, clamorous people bobbing back and forth in a state of apocalyptic merriment, but a table has been reserved for you and your friends, so you sit down at the table, and the moment your body makes contact with the chair you understand that you are depleted, drained of all physical energy, all emotional energy, utterly spent in a way you never could have imagined possible, so crushed that you feel you might burst into tears at any moment. You order a whiskey, and when you take hold of the glass and raise it to your lips, you are heartened to notice that your fingers can move again. You order a second whiskey, then a third whiskey, then a fourth whiskey, and suddenly you fall asleep. In spite of the frenzy all around you, you manage to go on sleeping until the good man who is your producer hoists you to your feet and half-drags you, half-carries you back to your hotel.

Yes, you drink too much and smoke too much, you have lost teeth without bothering to replace them, your diet does not conform to the precepts of contemporary nutritional wisdom, but if you shun most vegetables it is simply because you do not like them, and you find it difficult, if not impossible, to eat what you do not like. You know that your wife worries about you, especially about your smoking and drinking, but mercifully, until now, no X-ray has revealed any damage to your lungs, no blood test has revealed any devastation to your liver, and so you forge on with your vile habits, knowing full well that they will ultimately do you grave harm, but the older you become the less likely it seems that you will ever have the will or the courage to abandon your beloved little cigars and frequent glasses of wine, which have given you so much pleasure over the years, and you sometimes think that if you were to cut these things out of your life at this late date, your body would simply fall apart, your system would cease to function. No doubt you are a flawed and wounded person, a man who has carried a wound in him from the very beginning (why else would you have spent the whole of your adult life bleeding words onto a page?), and the benefits you derive from alcohol and tobacco serve as crutches to keep your crippled self upright and moving through the world. *Self-medication*, as your wife calls it. Unlike your mother's mother, she does not want you to be different. Your wife tolerates your weaknesses and does not rant or scold, and if she worries, it is only because she wants you to live forever. You count the reasons why you have held her close to you for so many years, and surely this is one of them, one of the bright stars in the vast constellation of enduring love.

Needless to say, you cough, especially at night, when your body is in a horizontal position, and on those nights when the breath tubes are excessively clogged, you climb out of bed, go into another room, and cough on madly until you have hacked up all the gunk. According to your friend Spiegelman (the most ardent smoker you know), whenever someone asks him why he smokes, he inevitably answers: "Because I like to cough."

1952. Five years old, naked in the bath, alone, big enough to wash yourself now, and as you lie on your back in the warm water, your penis suddenly springs to attention, popping out above the water line. Until this moment, you have seen your penis only from above, standing on your feet and looking down, but from this new vantage point, more or less at eye level, it occurs to you that the tip of your circumcised male organ bears a striking resemblance to a helmet. An old-fashioned sort of helmet, similar to those worn by firemen in the late nineteenth century. This revelation pleases you, since at that juncture of your life your greatest ambition is to grow up to become a fireman, which you consider to be the most heroic job on the face of the earth (no doubt it is), and how fitting that you should have a miniature fireman's helmet emblazoned on your very person, on the very part of your body, moreover, that looks like and functions as a hose.

The countless tight squeezes you have been in during the course of your life, the desperate moments when you have felt an urgent, overpowering need to empty your bladder and no toilet is at hand, the times when you have found yourself stuck in traffic, for example, or sitting on a subway stalled between stations, and the pure agony of forcing yourself *to hold it in*. This is the universal dilemma that no one ever talks about, but everyone has been there at one time or another, everyone has lived through it, and while there is no example of human suffering more comical that that of the bursting bladder, you tend not to laugh about these incidents until after you have managed to relieve yourself—for what person over the age of three would want to wet his pants in public? That is why you will never forget these words, which were the last words spoken to one of your friends by his dying father: "Just remember, Charlie," he said, "never pass up an opportunity to piss." And so the wisdom of the ages is handed down from one generation to the next.

Again, it is 1952, and you are in the backseat of the family car, the blue 1950 De Soto your father brought home the day your sister was born. Your mother is driving, and you have been on the road for some time now, going from where to where you can no longer remember, but you are on your way back, no more than ten or fifteen minutes from home, and for the past little while you have had to pee, the pressure in your bladder has been building steadily, and by now you are writhing on the backseat, legs crossed, your hand clamped over your crotch, uncertain whether you can hold out much longer. You tell your mother about your predicament, and she asks if you can hang in there for another ten minutes. No, you tell her, you don't think so. In that case, she says, since there's nowhere to stop between here and home, just go in your pants. This is such a radical idea to you, such a betrayal of what you consider to be your hard-won, manly independence, that you can scarcely believe what she has said. Go in my pants? you say to her. Yes, go in your pants, she says. What difference does it make? We'll throw your clothes in the wash the minute we get home. And so it happens, with your mother's full and explicit approval, that you pee in your pants for the last time.

Fifty years later, you are in another car, a rented car this time since you do not have one of your own, a spanking-new Toyota Corolla that you have been driving for the past three hours on your way back from Connecticut to your house in Brooklyn. It is August 2002. You are fifty-five years old and have been driving since you were seventeen, always with skill and confidence, known to everyone who has ever driven with you as *a good driver,* with no accident on your record beyond a single scraped fender in close to forty years behind the wheel. Your wife is up front with you in the seat to your right, and in the back is your fifteen-year-old daughter (who has just finished a summer acting program at a school in Connecticut), sprawled out asleep on the quilts and pillows that have served as her bedding for the past month. Also sleeping in the back is your dog, the ragged stray mutt you and your daughter brought home off the streets eight years ago, whom you dubbed Jack (after Jack Wilton, the hero of Nashe's *The Unfortunate Traveller*) and who has been a much loved if lunatic member of the household ever since. Your wife, who worries about many things, has never worried about your driving, and in fact has often complimented you on how well you handle yourself in various kinds of traffic:

passing other cars on multi-lane highways, for example, or negotiating the tangle of city streets, or easing your way around the twists and curves of backcountry roads. Today, however, she senses that something is wrong, that you are not concentrating properly, that your timing is slightly off, and more than once she has told you to watch what you are doing. You should know better by now than to doubt the wisdom of your wife's words, for she possesses an uncanny ability to read the minds of others, to see into the souls of others, to sniff out the hidden undercurrents of any human situation, and again and again you have marveled at how accurate her instincts have proven to be, but on this particular day her anxiety is so acute that it has begun to get on your nerves. Are you not a famously *good driver*? you tell her. Have you ever had an accident? Would you ever do anything to put the lives of the people you love most in the world at risk? No, she says, of course not, she doesn't know what has gotten into her, and once you reach the tollbooths at the Triborough Bridge, you say to her, Look, here we are, New York City, nearly home now, and after that she promises not to say another word about your driving. But something is wrong, even if you are not willing to admit it, for this is 2002, and so many things have happened to you in this year of grim surprises, why shouldn't your mastery of cars suddenly and inexplicably abandon you? Worst of all, there was your mother's death in mid-May (heart attack), which stunned you not because you didn't know that people of seventy-seven can and do die without warning but because she was in apparent good health, and just the day before the last day of her life, you talked to her on the phone, and she was in buoyant spirits, cracking jokes and telling such funny stories that after you hung up you said to your wife: "She hasn't sounded this happy in years." Your mother's death worst of all, but there was also the blood clot that formed in your left leg during a nine-hour coach flight to Copenhagen in early February, which kept you flat on your back for several weeks and forced you to walk with a cane for months afterward, not to speak of the trouble you have been having with your eyes, the tear in the cornea of your left eye to begin with, then the tear in the right cornea some weeks later, followed by repeated, altogether random instances in one eye or the other over the past several months, and the damage is always done in your sleep, which means there is nothing you can do to prevent it (since the cream prescribed by the ophthalmologist has had no effect), and on those mornings when you wake up with yet another torn cornea, the pain is ferocious, an eye being without question the most sensitive and vulnerable part of the body, and after you put in the painkilling drops the doctor has prescribed for such emergencies, it generally takes from two to four hours before the pain begins to disappear, and during those hours there is nothing you can do but sit still with a cold washcloth over the afflicted eye, which you keep shut, since opening that eye will make you feel as if a pin were being jabbed into it. A six-month siege of *coach leg*, then, and a chronic case of *dry eye*, and also the first full-blown panic attack of your life, which occurred just two days after your mother's death, followed by several others in the days immediately after that, and for some time now you have felt that you are disintegrating, that you, who were once nature's strongman, able to resist all assaults from within and without, impervious to the somatic and psychological travails that dog the rest of humanity, are not the least bit strong anymore and are rapidly turning into a debilitated wreck. Your family doctor has prescribed pills to keep the panic attacks under control, and perhaps those pills have been affecting your ability to drive this afternoon, but that seems unlikely to you, since you have driven with these pills in your system before, and neither you nor your wife ever noticed any difference. Impaired or not, you have now passed through the tollbooth at the Triborough Bridge and have begun the final stage of your journey home, and as you drive through the city you are not thinking about your mother or your eyes or your leg or the pills you swallow to keep your panic attacks at bay. You are thinking only about the car and the forty or fifty minutes it will take to reach your house in Brooklyn, and now that your wife has calmed down and no longer seems concerned about your driving, you are calm as well, and nothing out of the ordinary happens as you cover the miles from the bridge to the outskirts of your neighborhood. It is true that you have to pee, that your bladder has been sending out signals to you for the past twenty minutes, ever more rapid and dire signals of distress, and therefore you drive a little faster than perhaps you should, since you are doubly eager to get home, home for the sake of home, of course, and with it the relief of being able to emerge from the stuffy confines of the car, but also because getting home will allow you to run upstairs to the bathroom and relieve *yourself*, and yet even if you are pressing a little more than you should, all is well, and by now you are just two and a half minutes from the street where you live. The car is traveling down Fourth Avenue, an ugly stretch of dilapidated apartment buildings and empty warehouses, and because pedestrian traffic is sparse along these blocks, drivers rarely have to worry about anyone crossing the street, and on top of that the lights stay green for longer intervals than on most avenues, which encourages drivers to go fast, too fast, often far above the speed limit. This poses no problem if you are going straight ahead (that is why you have chosen this route, after all: because it will get you home more quickly than any other), but the onrush of traffic can make left turns somewhat perilous, since you must turn while the light is green, and while the light is green for you, it is also green for the cars speeding toward you from the opposite direction. Now, as you come to the juncture of Fourth Avenue and Third Street, where you must make the left turn that will take you home, you stop the car and wait for an opening, and suddenly you forget the lesson you learned from your father when he taught you how to drive close to forty years ago. He himself was a wretched, incompetent driver, an inattentive, daydreaming motorist who courted disaster every time he put his key in the ignition, but for all his shortcomings behind the wheel, he was an excellent teacher of others, and the best piece of advice he ever gave you was this: drive defensively; work on the assumption that everyone else on the road is stupid and crazy; take nothing for granted. You have always held these words uppermost in your thoughts, and they have served you well for all these years, but now, because you are desperate to empty your bladder, or because a pill has affected your judgment, or because you are tired and not paying close attention, or because you have turned into a *debilitated wreck,* you impulsively decide to take a chance, which is to say, to go on the offensive. A brown van is coming toward you. Going fast, yes, but no more than forty-five miles an hour, you think, fifty at most, and after gauging the distance of the van from where you have stopped in relation to the speed of the van, you are certain you will be able to make the left turn and get through the intersection without any problem—but only if you act quickly and step on the accelerator *now.* Your calculations, however, are founded on the belief that the van is traveling at forty-five or fifty miles an hour, which is in fact not true. It is going faster than that, at least sixty, perhaps even sixty-five, and therefore, once you make the left turn and begin hustling through the intersection, the van is suddenly and unexpectedly upon you, and since you are looking forward and not to your right, you do not see the van as it comes crashing into your car—a ninety-degree-angle hit, straight into the front door on the passenger's side, the side on which your wife is sitting. The impact is thunderous, convulsive, cataclysmic—an explosion loud enough to end the world. You feel as if Zeus has hurled a lightning bolt at you and your family, and an instant later the car is spinning, out of control, madly rotating down the street until it collides with a metal lamppost and comes to an abrupt and jarring halt. Then everything goes silent, the entire universe is enveloped in silence, and when at last you are able to think again, the first thought that comes to you is that you are alive. You look at your wife and see that her eyes are open, that she is breathing and therefore alive as well, and then you turn around to look at your daughter in the back, and she too is alive, jolted from the depths of sleep by the double blow of van and lamppost, sitting up and looking at you with large, bewildered eyes, her lips whiter than any lips you have ever seen, lips as white as the paper you are writing on now, and you understand that she has been saved by the quilts and pillows she was sleeping on, saved by the fact that one's muscles are utterly relaxed in sleep, and therefore no bones are broken, her head has not been hurled into contact with any hard surface, and she will be all right, is all right, as is the dog, who was sleeping on the quilts and pillows as well. Then you turn back to have another look at your wife, who was closest to the impact of the collision, and from the way she is sitting there beside you, so still, so mute, so absent from her surroundings, you fear that her neck might be broken, her long and slender neck, the beautiful neck that is the very emblem of her extraordinary beauty. You ask her how she is, if she feels any pain and if so where, but if she manages to answer you, her response is muffled, spoken in such a low voice that you cannot hear what she says. By now, you have become aware of noise outside the car, things are happening around you, several things at once, most noticeably the shrieking voice of the woman who was driving the van, who is hopping around in the street, angrily insulting you for causing the accident. (You will later learn that she was driving without a license, that the van did not belong to her, and that she had been in trouble with the police on several occasions—which would account for the vehemence of her anger, since she was afraid of running afoul of the law—but as she stands there shouting at you now, you are appalled by her selfishness, stunned that she does not even bother to ask if you and your family are all right.) As if to blot out the vicious behavior of this woman (who, to use your father's words, is both stupid and crazy), a small miracle then occurs. A man is walking down Fourth Avenue, the only pedestrian on a thoroughfare that normally has no pedestrians, and against all reason, all logic, all presumptions about how the world supposedly works, this man is dressed in hospital whites, he is a young doctor, a native of India with smooth brown skin and an exceptionally handsome face, and seeing what has just happened, he approaches your car and calmly begins talking to your wife. There is no glass in the window anymore, which allows him to lean in and talk to her in a low voice, his soothing Indian voice, and as you listen to him ask all the standard questions a neurologist would pose to a patient—What is your name? What is the date? Who is the president?—you understand that he is doing everything he can to keep her conscious, to keep her from lapsing into a state of profound shock. Given the impact of the crash, it does not surprise you that for the time being she can no longer see any colors, that the world in front of her eyes is visible only in black and white. The doctor, who is not an apparition, who is a real man (but how not to think of him as a divine spirit who has come to save your wife?), stays with her until the ambulance and emergency team arrive. You and your daughter and Jack have left the car by now, but your wife must not move, everyone is worried that her neck could be broken, and as you stand there watching the firemen cut open the right front door with an instrument known as *the jaws of life*, you study the demolished car and cannot comprehend why all of you are still breathing. The car looks like a squashed insect. All four tires are flat, splayed out, twisted, the passenger side is caved in, and the back, which you now realize is the part of the car that crashed into the lamppost, is crumpled up, with no glass left in the rear window. Slowly, the paramedics strap your wife onto a board to keep her immobilized, they slide her into an ambulance, you and your daughter are put in another ambulance, and then you all set out for the trauma unit at Lutheran Medical Center in Bay Ridge. After two CAT scans and a number of X-rays, the doctors announce that no bones are broken in your wife's back or neck. Happy, all of you happy, then, in spite of this brush with death, and as you leave the hospital together, your wife jokingly reports that the doctor in charge of conducting the CAT scans told her that she had the most perfect, most beautiful neck he had ever seen.

Eight and a half years have gone by since that day, and not once has your wife ever blamed you for the accident. She says the woman in the van was driving too fast and therefore was entirely responsible for what happened. But you know better than to exonerate yourself. Yes, the woman was driving too fast, but in the end that is of little consequence. You took a chance you shouldn't have taken, and that error of judgment continues to fill you with shame. That is why you vowed to quit driving after you left the hospital, why you have not sat behind the wheel of a car since the day you almost killed your family. Not because you don't trust yourself anymore, but because you are ashamed, because you understand that for one near-fatal moment you were just as stupid and crazy as the woman who crashed into you.

Two years after the crash, you are in the small French city of Arles, about to read from one of your books in public. Appearing with you will be the actor Jean-Louis Trintignant (a friend of your publisher's), who will take the passages you read in English and read them again in French translation. A double reading, as is customary in foreign countries where the audiences are not bilingual, with the two of you alternating from paragraph to paragraph as you march in tandem through the pages you have chosen for the event. You are glad to be in Trintignant's company tonight, since you hold his acting in great esteem, and when you think of the films you have seen him play in (Bertolucci's *The Conformist*, Rohmer's *Ma*

Nuit chez Maud, Truffaut's *Confidentially Yours*, Kieslowski's *Red*—to cite just some of your favorites), you are hard-pressed to come up with the name of another European actor whose work you admire more. You also feel tremendous compassion for him, since you know about the brutal, highly publicized murder of his daughter some years back, and you are keenly aware of the terrible suffering he has lived through, continues to live through. Like many of the actors you have known and worked with, Trintignant is a shy and reticent person. Not that he doesn't exude an aura of goodwill and friendliness, but at the same time he is closed in on himself, a man who finds talking to others difficult. At the moment, the two of you are together on stage rehearsing the evening's performance, alone in the large church or former church where the reading will be held. You are impressed by the timbre of Trintignant's voice, the resonance of his voice, the qualities of voice that distinguish great actors from merely good ones, and it gives you enormous pleasure to hear the words you have written (no, not quite your words, but your words translated into another language) conveyed through the instrument of that exceptional voice. At one point, apropos of nothing, Trintignant turns to you and asks how old you are. Fifty-seven, you say, and then, after a brief pause, you ask him how old he is. Seventy-four, he replies, and then, after another brief pause, you both go back to work. Following the rehearsal, you and Trintignant are taken to a room somewhere in the church to wait until the audience has been seated and the performance can begin. Other people are in the room with you, various members of the company that publishes your work, the organizer of the event, anonymous friends of people you don't know, perhaps a dozen men and women in all. You are sitting in a chair and not talking to anyone, just sitting in silence and looking at the people in the room, and you see that Trintignant, who is about ten feet away from you, is sitting in silence as well, looking down at the floor with his chin cupped in his hand, apparently lost in thought. Eventually, he looks up, catches your eye, and says, with unexpected earnestness and gravity: "Paul, there's just one thing I want to tell you. At fifty-seven, I felt old. Now, at seventy-four, I feel much younger than I did then." You are confused by his remark. You have no idea what he is trying to tell you, but you sense it is important to him, that he is attempting to share something of vital importance with you, and for that reason you do not ask him to explain what he means. For close to seven years now, you have continued to ponder his words, and although you still don't know quite what to make of them, there have been glimmers, tiny moments when you feel you have almost penetrated the truth of what he was saying to you. Perhaps it is something as simple as this: that a man fears death more at fifty-seven than he does at seventy-four. Or perhaps he saw something in you that worried him: the lingering traces of what happened to you during the horrible months of 2002. For the fact is that you feel more robust now, at sixty-three, than you did at fifty-five. The problem with your leg is long gone. You have not had a panic attack in years, and your eyes, which still act up every now and then, do so far less frequently than before. Also to be noted: no more car crashes, and no more parents for you to mourn.

Thirty-two years ago today, meaning half your life ago almost to the minute, the news that your father had died the previous night, another night in January filled with snow, just as this one is, the cold wind, the wild weather, everything the same, time moving and yet not moving, everything different and yet everything the same, and no, he did not have the luck to reach seventy-four. Sixty-six, and because you always felt certain that he would live to a ripe old age, there was never any urgency about clearing the fog that had always hovered between you, and therefore, as the fact of his sudden, unexpected death finally sank in, you were left with a feeling of unfinished business, the hollow frustration of words not spoken, of opportunities missed forever. He died in bed making love to his girlfriend, a healthy man whose heart inexplicably gave out on him. In the years since that January day in 1979, numerous men have told you that this is the best way to die (the little death turned into real death), but no woman has ever said it, and you yourself find it a horrible way to go, and when you think of your father's girlfriend at the funeral and the shell-shocked look in her eyes (yes, she told you, it was truly horrible, the most horrible thing she had ever lived through), you pray that such a thing never happens to your wife. Thirty-two years ago today, and you have gone on regretting that too-abrupt departure ever since, for your father did not live long enough to see that his blundering, impractical son did not end up in the poorhouse, as he always feared you would, but several more years would have been necessary for him to understand this, and it saddens you that when your sixty-six-year-old father died in his girlfriend's arms, you were still struggling on all fronts, still eating the dirt of failure.

No, you do not want to die, and even as you approach the age of your father when his life came to an end, you have not called any cemetery to arrange for your burial plot, have not given away any of the books you are certain you will never read again, and have not begun to clear your throat to say your good-byes. Nevertheless, thirteen years ago, just one month past your fiftieth birthday, as you sat in your downstairs study eating a tuna fish sandwich for lunch, you had what you now call your false heart attack, a siege of ever-mounting pain that spread through your chest and down your left arm and up into your jaw, the classic symptoms of cardiac upheaval and destruction, the dreaded coronary infarction that can stop a man's life within minutes, and as the pain continued to grow, to reach higher and higher levels of incendiary force, burning up your insides and setting your chest on fire, you grew weak and dizzy from the onslaught, staggered to your feet, slowly climbed the stairs with both hands clutching the banister, and collapsed on the landing of the parlor floor as you called out to your wife in a feeble, barely audible voice. She came running down from the top floor, and when she saw you there lying on your back, she took you in her arms and held you, asking where it hurt, telling you she would call the doctor, and as you looked up at her face, you were convinced you were about to die, for pain of that magnitude could only mean death, and the odd thing about it, perhaps the oddest thing that has ever happened to you, is that you weren't afraid, you were in fact calm and altogether accepting of the idea that you were about to leave this world, saying to yourself, This is it, you're going to die now, and maybe death isn't as bad as you had thought it was, for here you are in the arms of the woman you love, and if you must die now, consider yourself blessed to have lived as long as fifty years. You were taken to the hospital, kept overnight in an emergency room bed, given blood tests every four hours, and by the next morning the heart attack had become an inflamed esophagus, no doubt aggravated by the heavy dose of lemon juice in your sandwich. Your life had been given back to you, your heart was sound and beating normally, and on top of all that good news, you had learned that death was not something to be feared anymore, that when the moment comes for a person to die, his being shifts into another zone of consciousness, and he is able to accept it. Or so you thought. Five years later, when you had the first of your panic attacks, the sudden, monstrous attack that ripped through your body and threw you to the floor, you were not the least bit calm or accepting. You thought you were going to die then, too, but this time you howled in terror, more afraid than you had ever been in your life. So much for other zones of consciousness and quiet exits from this valley of tears. You lay on the floor and howled, howled at the top of your lungs, howled because death was inside you and you didn't want to die.

Snow, so much snow these past days and weeks that fifty-six inches have fallen on New York in less than a month. Eight storms, nine storms, you have lost track by now, and all through January the song heard most often in Brooklyn has been the street music made by shovels scraping against sidewalks and thick patches of ice. Intemperate cold (three degrees one morning), drizzles and mizzles, mist and slush, ever-aggressive winds, but most of all the snow, which will not melt, and as one storm falls on top of another, the bushes and trees in your back garden are all wearing ever-longer and heavier beards of snow. Yes, it seems to have turned into one of *those* winters, but in spite of the cold and discomfort and your useless longing for spring, you can't help admiring the vigor of these meteorological dramas, and you continue to look at the falling snow with the same awe you felt when you were a boy.

Roughhousing. That is the word that comes to you now when you think about the pleasures of boyhood (as opposed to the pains). Wrestling with your father, a rare circumstance since he was seldom present during the hours when you were awake (off to work while you were still asleep and home after you had been put to bed), but all the more memorable because of that perhaps, and the outlandish size of his body and muscles, the sheer bulk of him as you grappled in his arms and strove to defeat the King of New Jersey in hand-to-hand combat, and also your older cousin by four years, on those Sunday afternoons when you and your family visited your aunt and uncle's house, the same excessive physicality as you rolled around on the floor with him, the joy of that physicality, the abandon. Running. Running and jumping and climbing. Running until you felt your lungs would burst, until your side ached. Day after day and on into the evening, the long, slowly fading dusks of summer, and you out there on the grass, running for all you were worth, your pulse pounding in your ears, the wind in your face. A bit later on, tackle football, Johnny on the Pony, Kick the Can, King of the Castle, Capture the Flag. You and your friends were so nimble, so flexible, so keen on waging these pretend wars that you went at one another with unrelenting savagery, small bodies crashing into other small bodies, knocking one another to the ground, yanking arms, grabbing necks, tripping and shoving, anything and everything to win the game—animals the lot of you, wild animals through and through. But how well you slept back then. Switch off the lamp, close your eyes . . . and see you tomorrow.

More subtly, more beautifully, more gratifying in the long run, there was your ever-evolving skill at playing baseball, the least violent of sports, and the passion you developed for it beginning at six or seven years old. Catching and throwing, fielding ground balls, learning where to position yourself at each moment throughout the course of a game, depending on how many outs there were, how many runners were on base, and knowing in advance what you must do should the ball be hit in your direction: throw home, throw to second, try for a double play, or else, because you played shortstop, run into left field after a base hit and then wheel around to make the long relay throw to the correct spot on the field. Never a dull moment, in spite of what critics of the game might think: poised in a state of constant anticipation, ever at the ready, your mind churning with possibilities, and then the sudden explosion, the ball speeding toward you and the urgent need to do what must be done, the quick reflexes required to perform your job, and the exquisite sensation of scooping up a ground ball hit to your left or right and making a hard, accurate throw to first. But no pleasure greater than that of hitting the ball, settling into your stance, watching the pitcher go into his windup, and to hit a ball squarely, to feel the ball making contact with the meat of the bat, the very sound of it as you followed through with your swing and saw the ball flying deep into the outfield—no, there was no feeling like it, nothing ever came close to the exaltation of that moment, and because you became better and better at this as time went on, there were many such moments, and you lived for them in a way you lived for nothing else, all wrapped up in this meaningless boy's game, but that was the apex of happiness for you back then, the very best thing your body was able to do.

The years before sex entered the equation, before you understood that the miniature fireman between your legs was good for anything but helping you empty your bladder. It must be 1952 again, but perhaps a little earlier or a little later than that, and you ask your mother the question all children ask their parents, the standard question about where babies come from, meaning where did you come from, and by what mysterious process did you enter the world as a human being? Your mother's answer is so abstract, so evasive, so metaphorical that it leaves you utterly confounded. She says: The father plants the seed in the mother, and little by little the baby begins to grow. At this point in your life, the only seeds you are familiar with are the ones that produce flowers and vegetables, the ones that farmers scatter over large fields at planting time to start a new round of crops for harvest in the fall. You instantly see an image in your head: your father dressed as a farmer, a cartoon version of a farmer in blue overalls with a straw hat on his head, and he is walking along with a large rake propped against his shoulder, walking with a jaunty, insouciant stride out in some rural nowhere, on his way to *plant the seed*. For some time afterward, this was the picture you saw whenever the subject of babies was mentioned: your old man as a farmer, dressed in blue overalls with a ragged straw hat on his head and a rake propped against his shoulder. You knew there was something wrong about this, however, for seeds were always planted in the earth, either in gardens or in large fields, and since your mother was neither a garden nor a field, you had no idea what to make of this horticultural presentation of the facts of life. Is it possible for anyone to be more stupid than you were? You were a stupid little boy who lacked the wit to ask the question again, but the truth was that you enjoyed imagining your father as a farmer, enjoyed seeing him in that ridiculous costume, and when it comes right down to it, you probably wouldn't have understood what your mother was talking about if she had given you a more precise answer to your question.

Some weeks or months before or after this conversation with your mother, the little neighbor boy who smashed you on the head with the toy rake inexplicably went missing. His frantic mother rushed into your backyard and told you and your friends to start looking for him, and off you all went, thrashing into the borderland of wild shrubbery and tangled undergrowth that served as your secret hiding place, calling out the name of the boy, which was Michael, although he was commonly referred to as Brat or Monster—a midget felon whose life thus far had been devoted exclusively to acts of terrorism and violence. You entered a dense patch of bushes, flicking leaves out of your face and parting branches as you moved forward, fully expecting to find the runaway hoodlum huddled at your feet, but what you found instead was a nest of wasps or hornets, which you inadvertently stepped on, and seconds later you were engulfed by those stinging creatures, who were attacking your face and arms, and even as you tried to swat them away, others had crawled inside your clothes and were stabbing you in your legs and chest and back. Horrific pain. You went running out of the bushes onto the grass in the backyard, no doubt screaming your head off, and there was your mother, who took one glance at you and immediately began stripping off your clothes, and when there was no longer a stitch on you, she swooped up your naked body into her arms and ran with you toward the house. Once inside, she carried you upstairs, turned on the water, and put you in a cold, cold bath.

The boy was found. If you remember correctly, he was discovered in his own house, asleep on the living room floor, either hidden behind the sofa or curled up under a table, but if you need further proof that he did not die or vanish that day, you have only to recall the afternoon four or five years later when you were in bed with a case of the flu, one of those dreary sick days spent in the airless confinement of pajamas, fever, and aspirin tablets every four hours, thinking about your friends, who had already been let out of school and were no doubt playing a game of pickup baseball in Grove Park, since the sun was shining and the weather was warm, which made it an ideal afternoon for baseball. You were nine or ten years old, and as you remember it now, more than half a century later, you were the only person in the house. Outside in the backyard, chained to the wire runner your father had built for him, the family dog was dozing on the grass. He had been a part of your life for a good two years or longer, and you were intensely fond of him—a frisky young beagle with an appetite for adventure and a mad penchant for chasing after cars. He had already been run over once, injuring his left hind leg so badly that he could no longer use it, which had turned him into a three-legged dog, a strange, peg-legged kind of dog, a swashbuckling pirate of a dog in your opinion, but he had adjusted to his infirmity well, and even with just three legs he could still outrun any four-legged dog in the neighborhood. So there you were lying in bed in your upstairs room, certain that your crippled dog was safely tethered to his runner in the backyard, when a sudden volley of loud noises burst in on the quiet: a screech of tires in front of your house, immediately followed by a high-pitched howl of pain, the howl of a dog in pain, and from the sound of that dog's voice, you instantly knew that it was your dog. You jumped out of bed and ran outside, and there was the Brat, the Monster, confessing to you that he had unhooked your dog from his leash because he "wanted to play with him," and there was the man who had been driving the car, a much rattled and deeply upset man, saying to the people who had gathered around him that he had no choice, that the boy and the dog ran straight into the middle of the street, and it was either hit the boy or hit the dog, so he swerved and hit the dog, and there was your dog, your mostly white dog lying dead in the middle of the black street, and as you picked him up and carried him into the house, you told yourself no, the man was wrong, he should have hit the boy and not the dog, he should have killed the boy, and so angry were you at the boy for what he had done to your dog, you did not stop to consider that this was the first time you had ever wished that another human being were dead.

There were fights, of course. No one can get through boyhood without some of them, or many of them, and when you consider the tussles and confrontations you took part in, the bloody noses you both gave and received, the punches to the stomach that knocked the wind out of you, the inane headlocks and hammerlocks that sent you and your opponent sprawling to the ground, you can't think of a single instance when you were the one who started it, for you hated the whole business of fighting, but because there was always a bully somewhere in the vicinity, some brainless tough who would taunt you with threats and dares and insults, there were times when you felt compelled to defend yourself, even if you were the smaller one and were almost certain to be thrashed. You loved the mock wars of tackle football and Capture the Flag, the rough-and-tumble of barreling into a catcher at home plate, but real fighting made you sick. It was too fraught with emotional consequences, too wrenching in the angers it provoked, and even when you won your fights, you always felt like crying afterward. The slug-or-be-slugged approach to settling differences lost all appeal to you after a boy at summer camp came at you by jumping down from the rafters of the cabin and you wound up breaking his arm when you retaliated by slamming him into a wooden table. You were ten years old, and from that point on you steered clear of fighting as best you could, but fights continued to come your way from time to time, at least until you were thirteen, when you finally figured out that you could win any fight against any boy by kneeing him in the balls, by driving your knee into his crotch with all the force you could muster, and just like that, within a matter of seconds, the fight would be over. You acquired a reputation for being a "dirty fighter," and perhaps there was some truth to it, but you fought like that only because you didn't want to fight, and after one or two of these bouts, word got around and no one ever attacked you again. You were thirteen years old and had permanently retired from the ring.

No more battles with boys, but an abiding passion for girls, for kissing girls and holding hands with girls, something that started for you long before the onset of puberty, at a time when boys are supposedly not interested in such matters. As far back as the kindergarten class in which you fell for the girl with the golden ponytail (whose name was Cathy), you were always mad for kissing, and even then, at age five or six, you and Cathy would sometimes exchange kisses—innocent pecks, to be sure, but deeply pleasurable for all that. In those years of so-called latency, your friends were unanimous in their public scorn for girls. They would mock them, tease them, pinch them, and pull up their dresses, but you never felt that antipathy, could never rouse yourself to participate in these assaults, and all during that early grammar school period of your life (that is, up to the age of twelve, when you carried the American flag with a blood-soaked bandage around your head during your class's graduation ceremony), you continued to succumb to various infatuations with girls such as Patty, Susie, Dale, Jan, and Ethel. No more than kissing and holding hands, of course (you were physically incapable of having sex, the mechanics of which were still rather vague to you, since you did not arrive at full-fledged puberty until you were turning fourteen), but the kissing had become altogether ferocious by the time you reached graduation day. There were dances and unchaperoned parties in that final year before you entered junior high school, nearly every weekend you and a gang of fifteen or twenty others were invited to someone's house, and in those suburban living rooms and finished basements, impotent boys and girls with newly sprouting breasts would dance to the latest rock-and-roll songs (the hits of 1958 and 1959), and eventually, as the evening wore on, the lights would be dimmed, the music would stop, and girls and boys would pair off in hidden corners of the room, where they'd all neck crazily until it was time to go home. You learned much about lips and tongues that year, were indoctrinated into the pleasures of feeling a girl's body in your arms, of feeling a girl's arms wrapped around you, but that was as far as it went. There were lines that could not be crossed, and for now you were happy not to cross them. Not because you were scared, but because it never even occurred to you.

Finally, the day came when you went hurtling across the threshold that separates boyhood from adolescence, and now that you had felt the feeling, now that you had discovered that your old friend the fireman was in fact an agent of divine bliss, the world you lived in became a different world, for the ecstasy of that feeling had given a new purpose to your life, a new reason for being alive. The years of phallic obsession began. Like every other male who has wandered this earth, you were in thrall to the miraculous change that had occurred in your body. On most days, you could think of little else—on some days, of nothing else.

Nevertheless, when you recall the years immediately following your transformation, you are struck by how cautious and backward you were. In spite of your ardor, in spite of your constant pursuit of girls in junior and senior high school, the romances and flirtations with Karen, Peggy, Linda, Brianne, Carol, Sally, Ruth, Pam, Starr, Jackie, Mary, and Ronnie, your erotic adventures were frightfully tame and insipid, barely one step beyond the make-out sessions you took part in when you were twelve. Perhaps you were unlucky, or perhaps you weren't bold enough, but you tend to think it had more to do with the place and the time, a middle-class suburban town in the early sixties, and the unwritten code that girls did not give themselves to boys, that good girls had reputations to uphold, and the line was drawn at kissing and petting, notably the least dangerous form of petting, that is, the boy's hand placed on a breast covered by two or three layers of clothing, a sweater (depending on the season), a blouse, and a bra, but woe to the boy who tried to put his hand inside a blouse, let alone reach for the forbidden territory inside a bra, for that hand would be swiftly pushed away by the girl who had a reputation to uphold, even if that girl secretly wanted the hand to be there as much as the boy did. How many times were you rebuffed in this way, you wonder, how many useless expeditions did your hands make into the skirts and blouses of your companions, how many partial journeys toward the realm of bare skin before being turned back at the gates? Such were the impoverished conditions of your early erotic life. No bare skin allowed, no shedding of clothes, and forget, once and for all, that genitals have any part in the game you are playing. And so you and Linda go on kissing, kissing and then kissing some more, kissing until your lips are chapped and drool is sliding down your cheeks, and all the while you pray that the erection bulging in your pants will not explode.

You live in a torment of frustration and never-ending sexual arousal, breaking the North American masturbation record every month throughout the years 1961 and 1962, an onanist not by choice but by circumstance, trapped inside your ever-growing, ever-mutating body, the five-feet-two-inch thirteen-year-old now transformed into a five-feet-ten-inch fifteen-year-old, still a boy, perhaps, but a boy in a man's body, who shaves a couple of times a week, who has hair on his forearms and legs, hair under his arms, pubic hair because he is no longer pubescent but almost fully formed, and even as you forge on with your schoolwork and your sporting activities and travel ever more deeply into the universe of books, your life is dominated by your thwarted sexual hunger, you feel that you are actually starving to death, and no ambition is more important to you, no cause is more central to the well-being of your aching, starving self than to lose your virginity as quickly as possible. Such is your desire, in any case, but nowhere is it written that desires must be fulfilled, and so the torture goes on, all the way through the delirious abnegations of 1962 and on into the fall of 1963, when finally, at long long last, an opportunity presents itself, and although it is less than ideal, not at all what you have been imagining, you don't hesitate to say yes. You are sixteen years old. In July and August, you worked as a waiter at a summer camp in upstate New York, and the fellow who served as your partner, a funny, fast-talking kid from Queens (a city boy who knows his way around the New York streets—as opposed to you, who know next to nothing), calls to tell you that he has the address and telephone number of a brothel on the Upper West Side. He will make the appointment for you if you wish, and because you indeed wish, you take a bus into the city the following Saturday and meet your friend in front of an apartment building in the mid-Eighties, just off the river. It is a damp, drizzly afternoon in late September, everything is gray and sodden, umbrella weather, or at least a day for wearing hats, but you have neither an umbrella nor a hat, which is nevertheless fine, perfectly fine, since the last thing you are thinking about now is the weather. The word *brothel* has conjured up a host of enticing mental images for you, and you are expecting to walk into a large, sumptuously decorated establishment with red plush-velvet walls and a staff of fifteen or twenty alluring young women (what wretched film put *that* idea in your head?), but as you and your friend step into the elevator, which is the slowest, dirtiest, most graffiti-scarred elevator in all of New York, you quickly readjust your expectations. The luxurious brothel turns out to be a shabby little one-bedroom apartment, and only two women are there, the proprietress, Kay, a round black woman pushing fifty, who greets your friend with a warm hug, as if they are old familiars, and a much younger woman, also black, who appears to be around twenty or twenty-two. They are both sitting on stools in the tiny kitchen, which is separated from the bedroom by a thin curtain that doesn't quite touch the floor, both are dressed in colorful silk robes, and, much to your relief, the young one is highly attractive, with a very pretty face, perhaps even a beautiful face. Kay announces the price (fifteen dollars? twenty dollars?) and then asks you and your friend which one wants to go first. No, no, your friend laughs, he's just come along for the ride (no doubt the girls in Queens are less reluctant to shed their clothes than the girls in New Jersey), and so Kay turns to you and says that you can choose, either her or her young co-worker, and when you do not choose Kay, she does not appear to be offended—merely shrugs, smiles, puts out her hand, and says, "A little money, honey," at which point you dig into your pocket and pull out the fifteen or twenty dollars you owe her. You and the young one (too shy or too nervous, you forget to ask what her name is, which means that she has been nameless to you for all these years) step into the other room as Kay pulls the curtain shut behind you. The girl leads you toward the bed in the corner, she slips out of her robe and tosses it onto a chair, and for the first time in your life you are in the presence of a naked woman. A beautiful naked woman, in fact, a young woman with a remarkably beautiful body, with glorious breasts, glorious arms and shoulders, glorious backside, glorious hips, glorious legs, and after three long years of frustration and failure, you are beginning to feel happy, as happy as you have felt at any time since your adolescence began. The girl instructs you to take off your clothes, and then the two of you are on the bed together, both naked, and all you really want, at least for now, is to touch her and kiss her and feel the smoothness of her skin, which is marvelously smooth skin, so smooth that it makes you tremble just to put your hand on her, but kissing on the mouth is not part of the program, since prostitutes do not kiss their customers on the mouth, and prostitutes have no interest in foreplay, no interest in touching or being touched for the simple pleasure of touching and being touched, for sex under these circumstances is not pleasure but work, and the sooner the client can finish the job he has paid for, the better. She knows it is your first time, that you are an absolute novice with no experience whatsoever, and she treats you kindly and patiently, she is a good person, you feel, and if she wants to get down to the fucking part right away, no problem, you are more than willing to play by her rules, for there is no question that you are ready, that you have been sporting an erection from the instant you saw her take off the robe, and therefore, as she eases herself onto her back, you happily climb on top of her and let her guide your penis to the place where it has longed to be for so many years. Good, everything is good, it feels as good as you always imagined it would, no, even better, much better, and all is good for the first little while, when it seems only a matter of seconds before you will finish the job, but then you become aware of Kay and your friend talking and laughing in the kitchen, which is no more than ten or twelve feet from the bed, and once you become aware of them, you start to feel distracted, and as soon as your mind begins to wander from the task at hand, you can feel how bored the girl is, how tiresome this whole business is for her, and even though you are lying on top of her, she is nowhere near you, she is in another city, another country, and then, losing patience, she asks you if you can finish, and you say yes, of course, and twenty seconds later she asks you again and you say yes, of course, but the next time she speaks to you, she says: "Come on out and let me jerk you off. You young kids. You jerk off all the time, but when it comes to the real thing, you don't have a clue." And so you let her jerk you off, which is precisely what you have been doing to yourself for the past three years—with one small difference: better her hand than yours.

You never went back. For the next year and a half, you continued to wrangle with sweaters, blouses, and bras, went on kissing and stroking and struggling against the embarrassment of unseemly ejaculations, and then, at eighteen, you connived to skip out on the last two months of high school, first by coming down with a case of mononucleosis that kept you weak and bedridden for most of May, and then by heading to Europe on a student ship three weeks before your class graduated. You were allowed to do this by the school authorities because your grades were good and you had already been admitted to college for the fall, so off you went, with the understanding that you would return at the beginning of September to take your final exams and officially earn your diploma. Airplanes were an expensive way to travel in 1965, but student ships were not, and since you were operating on a tight budget (money earned from summer jobs over the past two years), you opted for the S.S. *Aurelia* and a slow, nine-day crossing from New York to Le Havre. Approximately three hundred students were on board, most of whom had already finished one or two years of college, meaning that most were a bit older than you, and with little or nothing to do as you and your fellow passengers inched your way across the Atlantic, filling the time with sleep, food, books, and films, it was only natural, altogether inevitable it seems to you now, that the thoughts of three hundred young people between the ages of eighteen and twenty-one should have been largely preoccupied with sex. Boredom and proximity, the languors of a fair-weather ocean voyage, the knowledge that the ship was a world unto itself and nothing that happened there could have any enduring consequences—all these elements combined to create an atmosphere of unguarded sensual ease. The dalliances began before the sun set on the first day, and they continued until the ship touched land two hundred hours later. It was a floating palace of fornication out there on the high seas, with couples slinking in and out of darkened cabins, boys and girls changing partners from one day to the next, and twice during the crossing you found yourself in bed with someone, each time with a sympathetic and intelligent girl, not unlike the good girls you had grown up with in New Jersey, but these girls were from New York, and therefore more sophisticated, more experienced than the hand-swatting virgins from your hometown, and because there was a strong attraction on both sides, in the first instance between you and Renée, in the second instance between you and Janet, there was no compunction about shedding clothes, about crawling between the sheets and making love in a way that had not been possible in that sad flat on the Upper West Side, with kissing and touching and genuine feeling now part of the adventure, and this was the real breakthrough, your initiation into the pleasure of two partners participating equally in the pleasures of prolonged intimacy. There was still much to learn, of course. You were no more than a beginner at that point, but at least you were on your way, at least you had discovered how much there was to look forward to.

Later on, when you were living in Paris in the early seventies, there were long stretches when you were alone, sleeping night after night with no body next to yours in the narrow bed of your small maid's room, and there were times when you became half-mad in your womanless solitude, not just from lack of sexual release but from lack of any physical contact, and because there was no one to turn to, no woman you could count on for the companionship you craved, you would sometimes go out and find yourself a prostitute, perhaps five or six times in the several years you lived there, wandering down the side streets of the now demolished neighborhood of Les Halles, which was just around the corner from your room, or else, venturing a bit farther, walk to the rue Saint-Denis and its adjacent alleys, passageways, and cobbled lanes, the sidewalks crowded with women lined up against the walls of buildings and the *hôtels de passe*, an array of feminine possibilities that ran the gamut from good-looking girls in their early twenties to harshly made-up street veterans in their mid-fifties, hookers representing every imaginable body type, every race and color, from rotund Frenchwomen to willowy Africans to voluptuous Italians and Israelis, some provocatively dressed in miniskirts with breasts spilling out of low-cut bras and flimsy blouses, others in blue jeans and modest sweaters, not unlike the girls you had gone to school with in your hometown, but all of them in high heels or boots, black or white leather boots, and around the neck an occasional boa or silk scarf, or an occasional S&M girl decked out in flamboyant leather garb, or an occasional pretend schoolgirl in a plaid skirt and prim white blouse, something to accommodate every desire and predilection, and walking down the middle of the carless streets, the men, an endless procession of silent men, examining the possibilities on the sidewalks with furtive glances or bold stares, all kinds of women prepared to hire themselves out to all kinds of men, from lonely Arabs to middle-aged johns in suits, the throngs of womanless immigrants and frustrated students and bored husbands, and once you joined those processions, you suddenly felt that you were no longer part of the waking world, that you had slipped into an erotic dream that was at once thrilling and destabilizing, for the thought that you could go to bed with any one of those women merely by offering her a hundred francs (twenty dollars) made you dizzy, physically dizzy, and as you prowled the narrow streets looking for a companion to satisfy the need that had driven you out of your room into this labyrinth of flesh, you found yourself looking at faces rather than bodies, or faces first and bodies second, searching for a pretty face, the face of a human being whose eyes had not gone dead, someone whose spirit had not yet entirely drowned in the anonymity and artificiality of whoredom, and strangely enough, on your five or six excursions into the thoroughly legal, government-sanctioned red-light districts of Paris, you generally managed to find one. No bad experiences, then, no encounter that filled you with regret or remorse, and when you look back on it now, you suppose you were well treated because you were not an aging man with a protruding belly or a foul-smelling laborer with dirt under his fingernails but an unaggressive, not unpresentable young man of twenty-four or twenty-five who made no idiosyncratic or uncomfortable demands on the women he went upstairs with, who was simply grateful not to be alone in his own bed. On the other hand, it would be wrong to classify any of these experiences as memorable. Brisk and forthright, goodwilled but altogether businesslike in execution, a service competently rendered for an allotted fee, but since you were no longer the bumbling sixteen-year-old neophyte of yore, that was all you ever expected. Still, there was one time when something unusual occurred, when a spark of reciprocity was ignited between you and your provisional consort, which happened to be the last time you ever paid a woman to sleep with you, the summer of 1972, when you were earning some much needed cash with a job as switchboard operator at the local bureau of the *New York Times*, the graveyard shift, roughly six P.M. to one A.M., you no longer remember the exact hours, but you would arrive when the office was emptying out for the day and sit there alone at a desk, the only person on the darkened floor of a building on the Right Bank, waiting for the telephone to ring, which it seldom did, and using the unbroken silence of those hours to read books and work on your poems. One weekday night when your shift was done, you left the office and stepped outside into the summer air, the warm embrace of the summer air, and because the Métro was no longer running, you started walking home, strolling south in the soft summer air, not at all tired as you ambled through the empty streets on the way back to your small, empty room. Before long you were on the rue Saint-Denis, where a number of girls were still working in spite of the late hour, and then you turned down a nearby side street, the one where the prettiest girls tended to congregate, understanding that you had no desire to go home just yet, that you had been alone for too long and dreaded going back to your empty room, and midway down the block someone caught your attention, a tall brunette with a lovely face and an equally lovely figure, and when she smiled at you and asked if you wanted company (*Je t'accompagne?*), you didn't think twice about accepting her offer. She smiled again, pleased by the quickness of the transaction, and as you continued to look at her face, you understood that she would have been a heart-stopping beauty if her eyes had not been too close together, if she had not been ever so slightly cross-eyed, but that was of no importance to you, she was still the most appealing woman who had ever walked this street, and you were disarmed by her smile, which was a magnificent smile in your opinion, and it occurred to you that if everyone in the world could smile as she did, there would be no more wars or human conflicts, that peace and happiness would reign on earth forever. Her name was Sandra, a French girl in her mid-twenties, and as you followed her up the winding staircase to the third floor of the hotel, she announced that you were her last customer of the night, and consequently there would be no need to rush, you could take as much time as you liked. This was unprecedented, a violation of all professional standards and protocols, but it was already clear to you that Sandra was different from the other girls who worked that street, that she lacked the hardness and coldness that necessarily seemed to go with the job. Then you were in the room with her, and everything continued to be different from all your previous experiences in this part of the city. She was relaxed, in a warm and expansive mood, and even when you both took off your clothes, even when you discovered how uncommonly beautiful her body was (*majestic* was the word that came to you, in the same way that the bodies of certain dancers can be called majestic), she was talkative and playful, in no hurry to get down to business, not at all put out by your desire to touch her and kiss her, and as she lolled on the bed with you, she began demonstrating the various lovemaking positions she and her friends used with their clients, the Kama Sutra of the rue Saint-Denis, twisting around and over and in on top of herself as she helped you contort your body into matching configurations, laughing softly at the absurdity of it all as she told you the name of each position. Unfortunately, you can remember only one of them now, which was probably the dullest one, but also the funniest because it was so dull: *le paresseux*, the lazy man, which was simply a matter of stretching out on your side and copulating with your partner face to face. You had never met a woman who was so at home in her body, so serene in the way she carried her naked self, and eventually, even though you wanted these demonstrations to go on until morning, you became too aroused to hold back any longer. You assumed that would be the end of it, *jouissance* had always been the end of it in the past, but even after you were finished, Sandra did not press you to leave, she wanted to lie on the bed with you and talk, and so you stayed with her for close to an hour more, happily encircled in her arms as your head rested on her shoulder, discussing things that have long since vanished from your mind, and when she finally asked what you did with yourself and you said that you wrote poems, you were expecting her to shrug with indifference or make some noncommittal remark, but no, no yet again, for once you started talking about poetry, Sandra closed her eyes and began to recite Baudelaire, long passages delivered with intense feeling and perfectly accurate recall, and you could only hope that Baudelaire had sat up in his grave and was listening.

> *Mère des souvenirs, maîtresse des maîtresses,*
> *O toi, tous mes plaisirs! ô toi, tous mes devoirs!*
> *Tu te rappelleras la beauté des caresses,*
> *La douceur du foyer et le charme des soirs,*
> *Mère des souvenirs, maîtresse des maîtresses!*

It was one of the most extraordinary moments of your life, one of the happiest moments of your life, and even after you were back in New York and the next chapter of your story was being written, you kept thinking about Sandra and the hours you had spent with her that night, wondering if you shouldn't jump on a plane, rush back to Paris, and ask her to marry you.

Always lost, always striking out in the wrong direction, always going around in circles. You have suffered from a lifelong inability to orient yourself in space, and even in New York, the easiest of cities to negotiate, the city where you have spent the better part of your adulthood, you often run into trouble. Whenever you take the subway from Brooklyn to Manhattan (assuming you have boarded the correct train and are not traveling deeper into Brooklyn), you make a special point to stop for a moment to get your bearings once you have climbed the stairs to the street, and still you will head north instead of south, go east instead of west, and even when you try to outsmart yourself, knowing that your handicap will set you going the wrong way and therefore, to rectify the error, you do the opposite of what you were intending to do, go left instead of right, go right instead of left, and still you find yourself moving in the wrong direction, no matter how many adjustments you have made. Forget tramping alone in the woods. You are hopelessly lost within minutes, and even indoors, whenever you find yourself in an unfamiliar building, you will walk down the wrong corridor or take the wrong elevator, not to speak of smaller enclosed spaces such as restaurants, for whenever you go to the men's room in a restaurant that has more than one dining area, you will inevitably make a wrong turn on your way back and wind up spending several minutes searching for your table. Most other people, your wife included, with her unerring inner compass, seem able to get around without difficulty. They know where they are, where they have been, and where they are going, but you know nothing, you are forever lost in the moment, in the void of each successive moment that engulfs you, with no idea where true north is, since the four cardinal points do not exist for you, have never existed for you. A minor infirmity until now, with no dramatic consequences to speak of, but that doesn't mean a day won't come when you accidentally walk off the edge of a cliff.

Your body in small rooms and large rooms, your body walking up and down stairs, your body swimming in ponds, lakes, rivers, and oceans, your body traipsing across muddy fields, your body lying in the tall grass of empty meadows, your body walking along city streets, your body laboring up hills and mountains, your body sitting down in chairs, lying down on beds, stretching out on beaches, cycling down country roads, walking through forests, pastures, and deserts, running on cinder tracks, jumping up and down on hardwood floors, standing in showers, stepping into warm baths, sitting on toilets, waiting in airports and train stations, riding up and down in elevators, squirming in the seats of cars and buses, walking through rainstorms without an umbrella, sitting in classrooms, browsing in bookstores and record shops (R.I.P.), sitting in auditoriums, movie theaters, and concert halls, dancing with girls in school gymnasiums, paddling canoes in rivers, rowing boats across lakes, eating at kitchen tables, eating at dining room tables, eating in restaurants, shopping in department stores, appliance stores, furniture stores, shoe stores, hardware stores, grocery stores, and clothing stores, standing in line for passports and driver's licenses, leaning back in chairs with your legs propped up on desks and tables as you write in notebooks, hunching over typewriters, walking through snowstorms without a hat, entering synagogues and churches, dressing and undressing in bedrooms, hotel rooms, and locker rooms, standing on escalators, lying in hospital beds, sitting on doctors' examination tables, sitting in barbers' chairs and dentists' chairs, doing somersaults on the grass, standing on your head on the grass, jumping into swimming pools, walking slowly through museums, dribbling basketballs in playgrounds, throwing baseballs and footballs in public parks, feeling the different sensations of walking on wooden floors, cement floors, tile floors, and stone floors, the different sensations of putting your feet on sand, dirt, and grass, but most of all the sensation of sidewalks, for that is how you see yourself whenever you stop to think about who you are: a man who walks, a man who has spent his life walking through the streets of cities.

Enclosures, habitations, the small rooms and large rooms that have sheltered your body from the open air. Beginning with your birth at Beth Israel Hospital in Newark, New Jersey (February 3, 1947) and traveling onward to the present (this cold January morning in 2011), these are the places where you have parked your body over the years—the places, for better or worse, that you have called home.

1. 75 South Harrison Street; East Orange, New Jersey. An apartment in a tallish brick building. Age 0 to 1½. No memories, but according to the stories you heard later in your childhood, your father managed to secure a lease by

giving the landlady a television set—a bribe made necessary by the housing shortage that hit the country after the end of World War II. Since your father owned a small appliance store at the time, the apartment you lived in with your parents was equipped with a television as well, which made you one of the first Americans, one of the first people anywhere in the world, to grow up with a television set from birth.

2. 1500 Village Road; Union, New Jersey. A garden apartment in a complex of low brick buildings called Stuyvesant Village. Geometrically aligned sidewalks with large swaths of neatly tended grass. *Large* is surely a relative term, however, given how small you were at the time. Age 1½ to 5. No memories, then some memories, then memories in abundance. The dark green walls and venetian blinds in the living room. Digging for worms with a trowel. An illustrated book about a circus dog named Peewee, a toy dalmatian who miraculously grows to normal size. Arranging your fleet of miniature cars and trucks. Baths in the kitchen sink. A mechanical horse named Whitey. A scalding cup of hot cocoa that spilled on you and left a permanent scar in the crook of your elbow.

3. 253 Irving Avenue; South Orange, New Jersey. A two-story white clapboard house built in the 1920s, with a yellow front door, a gravel driveway, and a large backyard. Age 5 to 12. The site of nearly all your childhood memories. You began living there so long ago, the milk was delivered by a horse-drawn wagon for the first year or two after you moved in.

4. 406 Harding Drive; South Orange, New Jersey. A larger house than the previous one, built in the Tudor style, awkwardly perched on a hilly corner with the tiniest of backyards and a gloomy interior. Age 13 to 17. The house in which you suffered through your adolescent torments, wrote your first poems and stories, and your parents' marriage dissolved. Your father went on living there (alone) until the day he died.

5. 25 Van Velsor Place; Newark, New Jersey. A two-bedroom apartment not far from Weequahic High School and the hospital where you were born, rented by your mother after she and your father separated and then divorced. Age 17 to 18. Bedrooms for your mother and little sister, but you slept on a fold-out couch in a minuscule den, not at all unhappy with the new arrangement, however, since you were glad your parents' painfully unsuccessful marriage was over, relieved that you were no longer living in the suburbs. You owned a car then, a secondhand Chevy Corvair bought for six hundred dollars (the same defective automobile that launched Ralph Nader's career—although you never had any serious trouble with yours), and every morning you would drive to your high school in not-too-distant Maplewood and go through the motions of being a high school student, but you were free now, unsupervised by adults, coming and going as you wished, getting ready to fly away.

6. Suite 814A, Carman Hall; Columbia University dormitory. Two rooms per suite, two occupants per room. Cinder-block walls, linoleum floors, two beds placed end to end under the window, two desks, a built-in cupboard for storing

clothes, and a common bathroom shared with the occupants of 814B. Age 18 to 19. Carman Hall was the first new dorm built on the Columbia campus in more than half a century. An austere environment, ugly and charmless, but nevertheless far better than the dungeonlike rooms to be found in the older dorms (Furnald, Hartley), where you sometimes visited your friends and were appalled by the stench of dirty socks, the cramped double-decker beds, the unending darkness. You were in Carman Hall during the New York City blackout of 1965 (candles everywhere, a mood of anarchic celebration), but what you remember best about your room are the hundreds of books you read there and the girls who occasionally wound up with you in your bed. The parietal rules of the all-male undergraduate college had been changed by the university administration just in time for the beginning of your freshman year, and females were now allowed into the rooms—with the door closed. For some time before that they had been allowed in if the door stayed open, followed by an interim period of a couple of years when the door could be left ajar by the width of a book, but then some brilliant boy with the mind of a Talmudic scholar challenged the authorities by using a matchbook, and that was the end of open doors. Your roommate was a childhood friend. He began dabbling in drugs midway through the first semester, became increasingly involved as the year wore on, and nothing you said to him ever made the smallest difference. You stood by helplessly and watched him disintegrate. By the next fall, he had dropped out of school—never to return. That was why you refused to dabble in drugs yourself, even as the Dionysian sixties roared around you. Alcohol yes, tobacco yes, but no drugs. By the time you graduated in 1969, two of your other boyhood friends were dead from overdoses.

7. 311 West 107th Street; Manhattan. A two-room apartment on the third floor of a four-story walkup between Broadway and Riverside Drive. Age 19 to 20. Your first apartment, which you shared with fellow sophomore Peter Schubert, your closest friend during your early days as an undergraduate. A derelict, ill-designed shit hole, with nothing in its favor but the low rent and the fact that there were two entrance doors. The first opened onto the larger room, which served as your bedroom and workroom, as well as the kitchen, dining room, and living room. The second opened onto a narrow hallway that ran parallel to the first room and led to a small cell in the back, which served as Peter's bedroom. The two of you were lamentable housekeepers, the place was filthy, the kitchen sink clogged again and again, the appliances were older than you were and hardly functioned, dust mice grew fat on the threadbare carpet, and little by little the two of you turned the hovel you had rented into a malodorous slum. Because it was too depressing to eat there, and because neither one of you knew how to cook, you tended to go out to cheap restaurants together for your meals, either Tom's or the College Inn for breakfast, gradually preferring the latter because of its excellent jukebox (Billie Holiday, Edith Piaf), and night after night dinner at the Green Tree, a Hungarian restaurant on the corner of Amsterdam Avenue and West

111th Street, where you subsisted on goulash, overcooked green beans, and savory *palačinka* for dessert. For some reason, your memories of what happened in that apartment are dim, dimmer than those of the other places you inhabited before and after. It was a time of bad dreams—many bad dreams—that you remember well (the Montaigne seminar with Donald Frame and the Milton course with Edward Tayler are still vivid) but all in all what comes back to you now is a feeling of discontent, an urgent desire to be somewhere else. The war in Vietnam was growing, America had split in half, and the air around you was heavy, barely breathable, suffocating. You signed up with Schubert for the Junior Year Abroad Program in Paris, left New York in July, quarreled with the director in August and quit the program, stayed on until early November as a non-student, an ex-student, living in a small, bare-bones hotel (no telephone, no private bathroom), where you felt yourself beginning to breathe again, but then you were talked into going back to Columbia, a sensible move given the draft and your opposition to the war, but the time off had helped you, and when you reluctantly returned to New York, the bad dreams had stopped.

8. 601 West 115th Street; Manhattan. Another oddly shaped two-room apartment just off Broadway, but in a far more solid building than the last one, with the further advantage of having a true kitchen, which stood between the larger room and the smaller room and was big enough (barely) to squeeze in a runty, drop-leaf table. Age 20 to 22. Your first solo apartment, continuously dark because of its location on

the second floor, but otherwise adequate, comfortable, sufficient to your needs of the moment. You spent your junior and senior years there, which were the wild years at Columbia, the years of demonstrations and sit-ins, of student strikes and police raids, of campus riots, expulsions, and paddy wagons carting off hundreds to jail. You diligently slogged through your course work, contributed film and book reviews to the student paper, wrote poems and translated poems, completed several chapters of a novel you eventually abandoned, but in 1968 you also participated in the weeklong sit-ins that led to your being thrown into a paddy wagon and driven downtown to a holding cell in the Tombs. As mentioned before, you had long since given up fighting, and you weren't about to tangle with the police when they smashed in the door of the room in Mathematics Hall where you and several other students were waiting to be arrested, but neither were you going to cooperate and walk out of there on your own two feet. You let your body grow limp—the classic strategy of passive resistance developed in the South during the civil rights movement—thinking the cops would carry you out of there without any fuss, but the members of the Tactical Patrol Force were angry that night, the campus they had invaded was turning into a bloody battleground, and they had no interest in your nonviolent, highly principled approach to the matter. They kicked you and pulled you by the hair, and when you still refused to climb to your feet, one of them stomped on your hand with the heel of his boot—a direct hit, which left your knuckles swollen and throbbing for days afterward. In the next morning's edition of the *Daily News,* there was a photograph of you being dragged off to the paddy wagon. The caption read *Stubborn Boy,* and no doubt that was exactly what you were at that moment of your life: a stubborn, uncooperative boy.

9. 262 West 107th Street; Manhattan. Yet another two-room apartment with a sit-down kitchen, but not oddly shaped as the others had been, a large room and a somewhat smaller room, but the small room was nevertheless ample, nothing like the coffin-sized spaces of the previous two. The top floor of a nine-story building between Broadway and Amsterdam Avenue, which meant more light than in any of the other New York apartments, but a shoddier building than the last one, with sluggish, haphazard maintenance by the cheerful super, a stout, barrel-chested man named Arthur. Age 22 to a couple of weeks past your 24th birthday, a year and a half in all. You lived there with your girlfriend, the first time either one of you had attempted cohabitation with a member of the opposite sex. The first year, your girlfriend was finishing her B.A. at Barnard and you were a graduate student in the Columbia doctoral program in comparative literature, but you were only biding your time, you knew from the start that you would last no longer than one year, but the university had given you a fellowship and a stipend, so you worked on your M.A. thesis, which turned into a sixty-page essay called "The Art of Hunger" (which examined works by Hamsun, Kafka, Céline, and Beckett), consulted from time to time with your thesis advisor, Edward Said, attended a number of mandatory seminars, skipped your lecture classes,

and went on writing your own fiction and poetry, some of which was beginning to be published in little magazines. When the year was over, you dropped out of the program as planned, quit student life forever, and went off to work on an Esso oil tanker that shuttled among various refineries in the Gulf of Mexico and along the Atlantic coast—a job with decent pay, which you were hoping would finance a temporary move to Paris. Your girlfriend found someone to share the expense of the apartment with her during the months you were gone: a quick-tongued, sharp-witted young white woman who earned her living pretending to be a black D.J. for an all-black radio station—with great success, apparently, which you found deeply amusing, but how not to see it as one more symptom of the times, another example of the nuthouse logic that had taken over American reality? As for you and your girlfriend, the experiment in conjugal living had been something of a disappointment, and after you returned from your stint in the merchant marine and started preparing for the trip to Paris, you both decided that the romance had played itself out and that you would make the trip alone. One night about two weeks before your scheduled departure, your stomach rebelled against you, and the pains that shot into your gut were so severe, so agonizing in their assault, so unrelenting as you lay doubled up on the bed, you felt as if you had eaten a pot of barbed wire for dinner. The only plausible explanation was a ruptured appendix, which you figured would have to be operated on immediately. It was two o'clock in the morning. You staggered off to the emergency room at St. Luke's

Hospital, waited in utmost misery for an hour or two, and then, when a doctor finally examined you, he confidently asserted that there was nothing wrong with your appendix. You were suffering from a bad attack of gastritis. Take these pills, he said, avoid hot and spicy foods, and little by little you'll begin to feel better. Both his diagnosis and his prediction were correct, and it was only later, many years later, that you understood what had happened to you. You were afraid—but afraid without knowing you were afraid. The prospect of uprooting yourself had thrown you into a state of extreme but utterly suppressed anxiety; the thought of breaking up with your girlfriend was no doubt far more upsetting than you had imagined it would be. You wanted to go to Paris alone, but a part of you was terrified by such a drastic change, and so your stomach went haywire and began to rip you in two. This has been the story of your life. Whenever you come to a fork in the road, your body breaks down, for your body has always known what your mind doesn't know, and however it chooses to break down, whether with mononucleosis or gastritis or panic attacks, your body has always borne the brunt of your fears and inner battles, taking the blows your mind cannot or will not stand up to.

10. 3, rue Jacques Mawas; 15th Arrondissement, Paris. Still another two-room apartment with a sit-down kitchen, on the third floor of a six-story building. Age 24. Not long after you arrived in Paris (February 24, 1971), you began having second thoughts about the breakup with your girlfriend. You

wrote her a letter, asking if she had the courage to try to make another go of it, and when she said yes, your good-and-bad, off-and-on, up-and-down relations with her continued. She would be joining you in Paris in early April, and in the meantime you went out to look for a furnished apartment (the ship had paid well, but not well enough to allow you to buy furniture), and you soon found the place on the rue Jacques Mawas, which was clean, filled with light, not too expensive, and equipped with a piano. Since your girlfriend was an excellent and devoted pianist (Bach, Mozart, Schubert, Beethoven), you took the apartment on the spot, knowing how pleased she would be by this lucky turn. Not just Paris, but Paris with a piano. You moved in, and once you had taken care of the household fundamentals (bedding, pots and pans, dishes, towels, silverware), you arranged for someone to come and tune the out-of-tune piano, which had not been played in years. A blind man showed up the next day (you have rarely met a piano tuner who is not blind), a corpulent person of around fifty with a dough-white face and eyes rolling upward in their sockets. A strange presence, you found, but not just because of the eyes. It was the skin, the blanched, puffball skin, which looked spongy and malleable, as if he lived underground somewhere and never let the light touch his face. With him was a young man of eighteen or twenty, who held on to his arm as he guided the tuner through the front door and on toward the instrument in the back room. The young man never said a word during the visit, so you failed to learn if he was a son, a nephew, a cousin, or a hired companion, but the tuner was a talkative fellow, and after he had completed his work, he paused for a while to chat with you. "This street," he said, "rue Jacques Mawas in the fifteenth arrondissement. It's a very small street, isn't it? Just a few buildings, if I'm not mistaken." You told him he wasn't mistaken, it was indeed a very small street. "It's funny," he continued, "but it turns out that I lived here during the war. It was a good place to find apartments back then." You asked him why. "Because," he said, "many Israelites used to live in this neighborhood, but then the war started and they went away." At first, you couldn't register what he was trying to tell you—or didn't want to believe what he was telling you. The word *Israelite* might have knocked you off balance a little, but your French was good enough for you to know that it was not an uncommon synonym for the word *juif* (Jew), at least for people of the war generation, although in your experience it had always carried a pejorative edge to it, not an outright declaration of anti-Semitism so much as a way of distancing the Jews from the French, of turning them into something foreign and exotic, that curious, ancient people from the desert with their funny customs and vengeful, primitive God. That was bad enough, but the next part of the sentence reeked of such ignorance, or such willful denial, that you weren't sure if you were talking to the world's biggest simpleton or a former Vichy collaborator. *They went away.* No doubt on a deluxe world cruise, an uninterrupted five-year holiday spent basking in the Mediterranean sun, playing tennis in the Florida Keys, and dancing on the beaches of Australia. You wanted the blind man gone, to remove him from your sight as quickly as possible, but as you were handing him his money, you couldn't resist asking one last question. "Oh," you said, "and where did they go when they went away?" The piano tuner paused, as if searching for an answer, and when no answer came, he grinned at you apologetically. "I have no idea," he said, "but most of them didn't come back." That was the first of several lessons that were hammered home to you in that building about the ways of the French—the next one being the War of the Pipes, which began a couple of weeks later. The plumbing equipment in your apartment was not new, and the chain-pull toilet with the overhead water tank was not in proper working order. Each time you flushed, the water would run for a considerable length of time and make a considerable amount of noise. You paid no attention to it, the running toilet was no more than a minor inconvenience to you, but it seemed that it created a great turbulence in the apartment below yours, the thunderous sound of a bath being drawn at full throttle. You were unaware of this until a letter was slipped under your door one day. It was from your downstairs neighbor, a certain Madame Rubinstein (how shocked the piano tuner would have been to learn that his wartime address still harbored some undead Israelites), an indignant letter complaining about the unbearable ruckus of midnight baths, informing you that she had written to the landlord in Arras about your carryings-on, and if he didn't begin eviction procedures against you at once, she would take the matter to the police. You were astonished by the violence of her tone, dumbfounded that she had not bothered to knock on your door and talk about the problem with you face to face (which was the standard method of resolving differences between tenants in New York apartment buildings) but instead had gone behind your back and contacted *the authorities*. This was the French way, as opposed to the American way—a boundless faith in the hierarchies of power, an unquestioning belief in the channels of bureaucracy to right wrongs and rectify the smallest injustices. You had never met this woman, had no idea what she looked like, and here she was attacking you with savage insults, declaring war over an issue that until then had escaped your notice. To avoid what you assumed would be immediate eviction, you wrote to the landlord, explained your side of the story, promised to have the malfunctioning toilet fixed, and received a jovial, thoroughly heartening letter in response: Youth must have its day, live and let live, no worries, but just go easy on the hydrotherapy, all right? (The nasty French as opposed to the good-natured French: in the three and a half years you lived among them, you met some of the coldest, meanest characters on the face of the earth, but also some of the warmest, most generous men and women you have ever known.) Peace reigned for a while. You still had not seen Madame Rubinstein, but the complaints from downstairs had stopped. Then your girlfriend arrived from New York and the silent apartment began to fill with the sounds of her piano playing, and because you loved music above all other things, it was inconceivable to you that anyone could object to the keyboard masterworks emanating from the third floor. One Sunday afternoon, however, an especially beautiful Sunday afternoon in late spring, as you sat on the couch listening to your girlfriend play Schubert's *Moments Musicaux,* a chorus of shrieking, irritated voices suddenly erupted downstairs. The Rubinsteins were entertaining guests, and what the angry voices were saying was: "Impossible! Enough! The last straw!" Then someone began whacking a broomstick on the ceiling directly below the piano, and a woman's voice cried out: "Stop! Stop that infernal racket now!" It was the last straw for you as well, and with the voice still screaming from the second floor, you burst out of your apartment, ran down the stairs, and knocked—knocked hard—on the Rubinsteins' door. It opened within three seconds (no doubt they heard you coming), and there you were, standing face to face with the formerly invisible Madame Rubinstein, who turned out to be an attractive woman in her mid-forties (why does one always want to suppose that unpleasant people are ugly?), and with no preamble of any kind, the two of you immediately launched into a full-bore shouting match. You were not someone who was easily agitated, you had little trouble keeping your temper under control, you would generally do anything possible to avoid an argument, but on that particular day you were beside yourself with anger, and because your anger seemed to lift your French to new levels of speed and precision, the two of you went at it as equals in the art of verbal combat. Your position: We have every right to play the piano on a Sunday afternoon, on any afternoon for that matter, at any time of any day of any week or month as long as the hour is not too early or too late. Her position: This is a respectable bourgeois house; if you want to play the piano, rent a studio; this is a good bourgeois house, and that means we follow the rules and behave in a civilized manner; loud noises are forbidden; when a police detective was living in your apartment last year, we had him thrown out of the building because he kept such irregular hours; this is a decent bourgeois house; we have a piano in our apartment, but do *we* ever play it? No, of course not. Her arguments struck you as lame, cliché-ridden tautologies, comic assertions worthy of Molière's Monsieur Jourdain, but she delivered them with such fury and venomous conviction that you were in no mood to laugh. The conversation was going nowhere, neither one of you would budge, you were building a wall of permanent animosity between you, and when you imagined how bitter the future would be if you kept on going at each other in this way, you decided the moment had come to pull out your trump card, to turn the dispute around and steer it in an entirely different direction. How sad it is, you said, how terribly sad and pathetic that two Jews should be fighting like this; think of all the suffering and death, Madame Rubinstein, all the horrors our people have been subjected to, and here we are shouting at each other over nothing; we should be ashamed of ourselves. The ploy worked just as you had hoped it would. Something about the way you said what you had said got through to her, and the battle was suddenly over. From that day forward, Madame Rubinstein ceased to be an antagonist. Whenever you saw her in the street or in the entranceway of the building, she would smile and address you with the formal propriety such encounters called for: *Bonjour, monsieur,* to which you would respond, politely smiling back at her, *Bonjour, madame.* Such was life in France. People pushed by force of habit, pushed for the pure pleasure of pushing, and they would go on pushing until you showed them you were willing to push back, at which point you would earn their respect. Add in the contingent fact that you and Madame Rubinstein were fellow Jews, and there was no reason to fight anymore, no matter how often your girlfriend played the piano. It sickened you that you had allowed yourself to resort to such an underhanded tactic, but the trump card had done its job, and it bought you peace for the rest of the time you lived on the rue Jacques Mawas.

11. 2, rue du Louvre; 1st Arrondissement, Paris. A maid's room (*chambre de bonne*) on the top floor of a six-story building facing the Seine. Age 25. Your room was in the back, and what you saw when you looked out the window was a gargoyle thrusting from the bell tower of the church next door—Saint-Germain l'Auxerrois, the same church whose bells tolled without interruption on August 24, 1572, ringing out the news of the Saint Bartholomew's Day massacre. When you looked to your left, you saw the Louvre. When you looked to your right, you saw Les Halles, and far off, at the northern edge of Paris, the white dome of Montmartre. This was the smallest space you have ever inhabited, a room so small that

only the barest essentials could fit in there: a narrow bed, a diminutive desk and straight-backed chair, a sink, and another straight-backed chair beside the bed, where you kept your one-burner electric hot plate and the single pot you owned, which you used for heating water to make instant coffee and boiled eggs. Toilet down the hall; no shower or bath. You lived there because you were low on money and the room had been given to you for free. The agents of this extraordinary act of generosity were your friends Jacques and Christine Dupin (the very best and kindest of friends—may their names be hallowed forever), who lived downstairs in a large apartment on the second floor, and because this was a Haussmann-era building, their apartment came with an extra room for a maid on the top floor. You lived alone. Once again, you and your girlfriend had failed to make a go of it, and once again you had split up. She was living in the west of Ireland by then, sharing a turf-heated cottage with a high school friend a few miles outside of Sligo, and although you went to Ireland at one point to try to win her back, your gallant gesture went for naught, since her heart had become entangled with that of a young Irishman, and you had walked in at an early juncture of their affair (which eventually came to naught as well), meaning that you had mistimed your trip, and you left the green, windy hills of Sligo wondering if you would ever see her again. You returned to your room, to the loneliness of your room, that smallest of small rooms that sometimes drove you out in search of prostitutes, but it would be wrong to say you were unhappy there, for you had no trouble adjusting to your reduced circumstances, you found it invigorating to learn that you could get by on almost nothing, and as long as you were able to write, it made no difference where or how you lived. Day after day throughout the months you were there, construction crews worked directly across from your building, digging an underground parking garage four or five levels deep. At night, whenever you went to your window and looked down at the excavated earth, at the vast hole spreading in the ground below you, you would see rats, hundreds of wet, gleaming rats running through the mud.

12. 29, rue Descartes; 5th Arrondissement, Paris. Another two-room apartment with a sit-down kitchen, on the fourth floor of a six-story building. Age 26. A number of well-paying freelance jobs had lifted you out of penury, and your finances were now robust enough for you to sign a lease on another apartment. Your girlfriend had returned from Sligo, the Irishman was no longer in the picture, and once again the two of you decided to join forces and take another stab at living together. This time, things went fairly smoothly, not without some bumps along the way, perhaps, but less jolting ones than previously, and neither one of you threatened to walk out on the other. The apartment at 29, rue Descartes was surely the most pleasant space you occupied in Paris. Even the concierge was pleasant (a pretty young woman with short blonde hair who was married to a cop, always smiling, always with a friendly word, unlike the snooping, ill-tempered crones who traditionally managed Paris apartment buildings), and you were glad to be living in this part of town, the middle of the

old Latin Quarter, just up the hill from the place de la Contrescarpe, with its cafés, restaurants, and vivid, boisterous, theatrical open-air market. But the good freelance jobs of the past year were drying up, and once again your resources were dwindling. You figured you would be able to hang on until the end of the summer, and then you would have to pack it in and return to New York. At the last minute, however, your stay in France was unexpectedly prolonged.

13. Saint Martin; Moissac-Bellevue, Var. A farmhouse in southeastern Provence. Two stories, immensely thick stone walls, red-tile roof, dark green shutters and doors, several acres of surrounding fields flanked by a national forest on one side and a dirt road on the other: the middle of nowhere. One of the stones above the front door was engraved with the words *L'An VI*—year six—which you took to mean the sixth year of the revolution, suggesting that the house was built in 1794 or 1795. Age 26 to 27. You and your girlfriend spent nine months as caretakers of that remote southern property, living there from early September 1973 to the end of May 1974, and although you have already written about some of the things that happened to you in that house (*The Red Notebook,* Story No. 2), there was much that you did not talk about in those five pages. When you think about the time you spent in that part of the world now, what comes back to you first is the air, the scents of thyme and lavender that rose up around you whenever you walked through the fields that bordered the house, the redolent air, the muscular air when the wind was blowing, the languorous air when the sun

lowered itself into the valley and lizards and salamanders crawled out from crevices in the stones to drowse in the heat, and then the dryness and roughness of the country, the gray, molten rocks, the chalky white soil, the red earth along certain paths and stretches of road, the scarab beetles in the forest pushing their mountainous spheres of dung, the magpies swooping over the fields and neighboring vineyards, the flocks of sheep that passed through the meadow just beyond the house, the sudden apparitions of sheep, hundreds of sheep bunched together and moving forward with the clattering sounds of their bells, the violence of the mistrals, the windstorms that would last for seventy-two unbroken hours, shaking every window, every shutter, every door and loosened tile of the house, the yellow broom that covered the hillsides in spring, the flowering almond tress, the rosemary bushes, the scrubby, stunted live oaks with gnarled trunks and shimmering leaves, the frigid winter that forced you to close off the second floor of the house and live in the three downstairs rooms, warmed by an electric heater in one and a wood fire in another, the ruins of the chapel on a nearby cliff where the Knights Templar used to stop on their way to fight in the Crusades, the static coming through your enfeebled transistor radio in the middle of the night for two weeks running as you strained to listen to the U.S. Armed Forces broadcasts from Frankfurt of the Mets versus Cincinnati in the National League play-offs, the Mets versus Oakland in the World Series, and then the hailstorm you were thinking about the other day, the icy stones hammering against the terra-cotta roof and melting on the grass around the house, not as large as baseballs, perhaps, but golf balls for nine-foot men, followed by the one time it snowed and everything briefly turned white, and your nearest neighbor, a bachelor tenant farmer living alone with his truffle dog in a crumbling yellow house and dreaming of world revolution, the shepherds drinking in the hilltop bar of Moissac-Bellevue, their hands and faces black with dirt, the dirtiest men you have ever seen, and everyone speaking with the rolling *r*'s of the southern French accent, the added *g*'s that turned the words for wine and bread into *vaing* and *paing*, the *s*'s dropped elsewhere in France still surviving their Provençal origins, turning *étrangers* into *estrangers* (strangers, foreigners), and all through the region the rocks and walls painted with the slogan *Occitanie Libre!*, for this was the medieval land of *oc* and not of *oui*, and yes, you and your girlfriend were *estrangers* that year, but how much softer life was in this part of the country when compared to the brittle formalities and edginess of Paris, and how warmly you were treated during your time in the south, even by the stuffy, bourgeois couple with the impossible name of Assier de Pompignon, who would occasionally invite you to their house in the adjacent village of Régusse to watch films on TV, not to mention the people you came to know in Aups, seven kilometers from the house, where you went on your twice-weekly shopping expeditions, a town of three or four thousand people that came to feel like a vast metropole as the months of isolation rolled on, and because there were only two principal cafés in Aups, the right-wing café and the left-wing café, you frequented the left-wing café, where you were welcomed in by the regulars, the scruffy farmers and mechanics who were either Socialists or Communists, the rowdy, talkative locals who grew increasingly fond of the young American *estrangers*, and you remember sitting with them in that bar as you all watched the 1974 presidential election returns on TV, the campaign between Giscard and Mitterrand following Pompidou's death, the hilarity and ultimate disappointment of that evening, everyone soused and cheering, everyone soused and cursing, but also in Aups there was your friend the butcher's son, more or less your age, who worked in his father's shop and was being groomed to take over the business, but at the same time a passionate and highly skilled photographer, who spent that year documenting the evacuation and demolition of a small village that was scheduled to be inundated for the construction of a dam, the butcher's son with his heartbreaking photographs, the drunken men in the Socialist/Communist bar, but also the dentist in Draguignan, the man your girlfriend had to visit again and again for the complicated root-canal work he performed on her, all the many hours she spent in his chair, and when the work was finally done and he presented her with the bill, it came to all of three hundred francs (sixty dollars), a sum so low, so incommensurate with the time and effort he had expended on her, that she asked him why he had charged her so little, to which he responded, with a wave of the hand and a diffident little shrug, "Forget it. I was young once myself."

14. 456 Riverside Drive; in the middle of the long block

between West 116th Street and West 119th Street, Manhattan. Two rooms with a razor-thin galley kitchen between them, the northern penthouse or tenth floor of a nine-story building overlooking the Hudson. *Penthouse* was a deceptive term in this case, since your apartment and the southern penthouse next to it were not a structural part of the building you lived in. PHN and PHS were located inside a separate, freestanding, flat-roofed, diminutive one-story house built out of white stucco, which sat on the main roof like a peasant hut incongruously transported from the back street of a Mexican village. Age 27 to 29. The interior space was cramped, barely adequate for two people (you and your girlfriend were still together), but affordable New York apartments turned out to be scarce, and after your return from three and a half years abroad, you spent more than a month looking for somewhere to live, anywhere to live, and you felt fortunate to have landed in this airy if too crowded perch. Brilliant light, gleaming hardwood floors, fierce winds blowing off the Hudson, and the singular gift of a large L-shaped roof terrace that equaled or surpassed the square footage of the apartment inside. In warm weather, the roof mitigated the effects of claustrophobia, and you never tired of going out there and looking at the view from the front of the building: the trees of Riverside Park, Grant's Tomb to the right, the traffic cruising along the Henry Hudson Parkway, and most of all the river, with its spectacle of unceasing activity, the countless numbers of boats and sailing vessels that traveled along its waters, the freighters and tugs, the barges and yachts and cabin cruisers, the daily regatta of industrial ships and pleasure craft that populated the river, which you soon discovered was another world, a parallel world that ran beside the patch of land you inhabited, a city of water just beyond the city of stones and earth. A stray hawk would settle onto the roof every now and then, but most often you were visited by gulls, crows, and starlings. One afternoon, a red pigeon landed outside your window (salmon-colored, speckled with white), a wounded fledgling with fearless curiosity and strange, red-rimmed eyes, and after you and your girlfriend fed him for a week and he was well enough to fly again, he kept coming back to the roof of your apartment, nearly every day for months, so often that your girlfriend eventually gave him a name, Joey, which meant that Joey the pigeon had acquired the status of pet, an outdoor companion who shared his address with you until the following summer, when he flapped his wings one last time and flew away for good. Early on: working from noon to five for a rare-book dealer on East Sixty-ninth Street, writing poems, reviewing books, and slowly reacclimating yourself to America, just as the country was living through the Watergate hearings and the fall of Richard Nixon, which made it a slightly different America from the one you had left. On October 6, 1974, about two months after you moved in, you and your girlfriend were married. A small ceremony held in your apartment, then a party thrown by a friend who lived in a nearby apartment that was much larger than yours. Given the frequent changes of heart that had afflicted the two of you from the beginning, the constant comings and goings, the affairs with other people, the breakups and makeups that followed one another as regularly as the changing of the seasons, the thought that either one of you should have considered marriage at this point now strikes you as an act of delusional folly. At the very least you were taking an enormous risk, gambling on the solidity of your friendship and your shared ambitions as writers to make marriage into something different from what you had already experienced together, but you lost the bet, you both lost because you were destined to lose, and therefore you managed to keep it going for only four years, marrying in October 1974 and calling it quits in November 1978. You were both twenty-seven when you took your vows, old enough to know better, perhaps, but at the same time neither one of you was anywhere close to full adulthood, you were both still adolescents at the core, and the hard truth was that you didn't have a chance.

15. 2230 Durant Avenue; Berkeley, California. A small efficiency apartment (two rooms and a kitchenette) across from the college football stadium, within walking distance of the university campus. Age 29. Restless, dissatisfied for no reason you could name, feeling ever more hemmed in by the too-tiny apartment in New York, you were rescued by a sudden infusion of cash (a grant from the Ingram Merrill Foundation), which opened the door to other possibilities, other solutions to the problem of how and where to live, and since you felt the moment had come to shake things up for yourself, you and your first wife boarded a train in New York, traveled to Chicago, where you disembarked and switched to

another train, and then headed for the West Coast, passing through the interminable flatlands of Nebraska, the Rockies, the deserts of Utah and Nevada, and pulled into San Francisco after a three-day journey. It was April 1976. The idea was to test out California for half a year and see if you might not want to move there permanently. You had several good friends in the area, you had visited the previous year and had come away with a favorable impression, and if you chose to conduct your experiment in Berkeley rather than in San Francisco, it was because the rents were lower there and you didn't have a car, and life without a car would be more manageable on that side of the Bay. The apartment wasn't much of anything, a low-ceilinged box with a faint odor of mildew and mold when the windows were shut, but not unlivable, not grim. You have no memory of making the decision to rent it, however, because not long after you arrived in town, sometime during the first week, when you were temporarily staying with friends, you were invited to play in a pickup softball game, in the second inning of which, with your back turned to the runner as you stood well out of the baseline waiting for a throw from the outfield, the runner intentionally went out of his way to crash into you from behind, leveling you with a murderous football block (wrong sport), and because he was a large man and you were not prepared for the blow, the collision snapped your head back before you fell to the ground, which caused a severe case of whiplash. (Your attacker, known for his bad sportsmanship and often referred to as "the Animal," was a highly sophisticated intellectual who went on to write books about seventeenth-century Dutch painting and translate a number of German poets. He turned out to be a former student of a former professor of yours, a man much admired by both of you, and when the Animal was informed of the connection, he was deeply contrite, saying he never would have run into you if he had known who you were. You have always been mystified by this apology. Was he trying to tell you that only former students of Angus Fletcher's were exempt from his dirty tactics but all others were fair game? You continue to scratch your head in wonder.) Your friends took you to the emergency room of the local hospital, where you were given a padded, Velcro-adjustable neck brace and a prescription for heavy doses of the muscle relaxant Valium, a drug you had never taken and which you hope you will never have to take again, for efficient as it was in alleviating the pain, it put you in a mindless stupor for the better part of a week, obliterating the memory of events an instant after those events occurred, meaning that several days of your life have been removed from the calendar. You cannot bring back a single thing that happened to you while you were walking around in your Frankenstein-monster neck brace and swallowing those amnesia-inducing pills, and therefore, when you and your first wife moved into the apartment on Durant Avenue, you praised her for having found such conveniently located digs, even though she had consulted with you at length before you both made the decision to live there. You stayed for the six months you had allotted yourselves, but no more. California had much to recommend it, and you fell in love with the landscape, the vegetation, the ever-present aroma of eucalyptus in the air, the fogs and all-encompassing showers of light, but after a while you found yourself missing New York, the vastness and confusion of New York, for the better you came to know San Francisco, the smaller and duller it seemed to you, and while you had no problem living in remotest seclusion (the nine months in the Var, for example, which had been an intensely fertile time for you), you decided that if you were going to live in a city, it had to be a big city, the biggest city, meaning that you could embrace the extremes of far-flung rural places and massive urban places, both of which seemed inexhaustible to you, but small cities and towns used themselves up too quickly, and in the end they left you cold. So you went back to New York in September, reclaimed the little apartment overlooking the Hudson (which had been rented out to a subtenant), and dug in again. But not for long. In October, the good news, the much-hoped-for news that a child was on the way—which meant that you would have to find another place to live. You wanted to stay in New York, you fully expected to stay in New York, but New York was too expensive, and after several months of searching for a larger apartment that you could afford, you accepted defeat and started looking elsewhere.

16. 252 Millis Road; Stanfordville, New York. A white, two-story house in northern Dutchess County. Construction

date unknown, but neither new nor particularly old, which would suggest sometime between 1880 and 1910. Half an acre of land, with a vegetable garden in back, a dark, pine-shaded yard in front, and a small patch of woods between your property and the one to the south. A worn-out but not altogether decrepit place, something to be improved on over time if sufficient funds were available, with a living room, dining room, kitchen, and guest room/study on the ground floor and three bedrooms upstairs. Purchase price: $35,000. One of several houses on a rural side road with moderate traffic. Not the extreme isolation of Provence, but a life in the country for all that, and if you never ran into altruistic dentists or left-wing farmers, your neighbors on Millis Road were kind, solid citizens, many of them young couples with small children, all of whom you came to know to one degree or another, but what you remember best about your Dutchess County neighbors are the tragedies that took place in those houses, the twenty-eight-year-old woman who came down with M.S., for example, or the grieving middle-aged couple next door whose twenty-five-year-old daughter had died of cancer within the past year, the mother now reduced to skin and bone from a steady diet of gin and her tender husband doing his best to prop her up, so much suffering behind the locked doors and drawn shades of those houses, and among those houses your own house must be included as well. Age 30 to 31. A bleak time, without question the bleakest time you have ever gone through, brightened only by the birth of your son in June 1977. But that was the place where your first marriage broke apart, where you were overwhelmed by constant money problems (as described in *Hand to Mouth*), and you came to a dead end as a poet. You don't believe in haunted houses, but when you look back on that time now, you feel that you were living under an evil spell, that the house itself was partly to blame for the troubles that descended on you. For many decades before you moved in, the owners had been a pair of unmarried sisters, German-Americans named Stemmerman, and by the time you bought the place from them, they were exceedingly old, in their late eighties or early nineties, one blind and the other deaf, and both had been in a nursing home for close to a year. A neighbor who lived a couple of doors down the road handled the negotiations for them—a vivacious woman who had been born in Cuba, was married to a quiet American auto mechanic, and collected glass figurines of elephants (!?)—and she told you a number of stories about the notorious Stemmerman sisters, who apparently hated each other and had been locked in mortal combat since childhood, the two of them bound together for life and yet bitter enemies to the last, who were known to engage in such loud, vicious quarrels that their voices could be heard up and down the length of Millis Road. When the neighbor started talking about how the deaf sister would punish the blind sister by locking her in the downstairs closet, you couldn't help conjuring up scenes from Gothic novels and remembering that tacky black-and-white movie with Bette Davis and Joan Crawford from the early sixties. How amusing, you thought, a couple of grotesque and crazy characters, but that's all in the past now, you and your pregnant wife would be bringing youth and vigor to the old house, and everything was about to change—all the while neglecting to consider that the Stemmermans had lived there for fifty or sixty years, perhaps seventy or eighty years, and that every inch of the house was impregnated with their malevolent spirits. You actually met the deaf sister one day at the Cuban woman's house (she nearly choked to death trying to drink a cup of tepid coffee), but she seemed benign enough to you, and you didn't give the matter another thought. Then you moved in, and in those early days of cleaning and rearranging furniture (some of which came with the house), you and your first wife pulled an armoire away from the wall in the upstairs hallway and found a dead crow on the floor behind it—a long-dead crow, utterly desiccated but intact. No, that wasn't amusing, not amusing at all, and even though you both tried to laugh it off, you went on thinking about that dead bird for months afterward, that dead black bird, the classic omen of bad tidings. The next morning, you discovered two or three boxes of books on the back porch, and because you were curious to see if anything was worth holding on to, you opened the boxes. One by one, you pulled out pamphlets from the John Birch Society, paperback books about the Communist plot to infiltrate the United States government, several volumes about the fluoride conspiracy to brainwash American children, pro-Nazi tracts published in English before the war, and then, most disturbing of all, a copy of *The Protocols of the Elders of*

Zion, the book of books, the most repellent and influential defense of anti-Semitism ever written. You had never thrown away a book, had never been tempted to throw away a book, but these books you threw away, driving the boxes to the town dump and purposefully shoving them under a mound of rotting garbage. It wasn't possible to live in a house with such books in it. You hoped that would be the end of the story, but even after you got rid of the books, it still wasn't possible to live there. You tried, but it simply wasn't possible.

17. 6 Varick Street; Manhattan. One room on the top floor of a ten-story industrial building in what is now known as Tribeca. A sub-sublet, passed on to you by the sometime girlfriend of a childhood friend of yours. One hundred dollars a month for the privilege of camping out in a former electrical supply office, a gutted shell not meant for human habitation, which until recently had served as a storage room for the artist's loft across the hall. A cold-water sink, but no bath, toilet, or kitchen facilities. Living conditions not unlike those in your maid's room on the rue du Louvre in Paris, but this room was three or four times larger than that one—as well as three or four times dirtier. Age 32. Before landing there in early 1979, a whirlwind of shocks, sudden changes, and inner upheavals that turned you around and set your life on a different course. With nowhere to go and no money to finance a move even if you had known where to go, you stayed on in the Dutchess County house after the breakup of your marriage, sleeping on the sofa bed in the corner of your downstairs

study, which you now realize (thirty-two years later) had been your bed as a child. A couple of weeks later, on a trip down to New York, you experienced the revelation, the scalding, epiphanic moment of clarity that pushed you through a crack in the universe and allowed you to start writing again. Three weeks after that, immersed in the prose text you had begun immediately after your resuscitation, your liberation, your new beginning, the unexpected hammer blow of your father's death. To your first wife's infinite credit, she stuck with you through the dismal days and weeks that followed, the ordeal of funeral arrangements and estate matters, disposing of your father's neckties, suits, and furniture, taking care of the sale of his house (which had already been in the works), standing by you through all the wrenching, practical business that follows death, and because you were no longer married, or married in name only, the pressures of marriage had been lifted, and once again you were friends, much as you had been in your early days together. You started writing the first part of *The Invention of Solitude*. By the time you moved to Varick Street in early spring, you were well into it.

18. 153 Carroll Street; Brooklyn. A railroad flat on the third floor of a four-story building near Henry Street. Age 33 to 34. Three rooms, sit-down kitchen, and bathroom. The bedroom, overlooking the street in front, was large enough to fit in a double bed for yourself and a single bed for your son (the same sofa bed you had used as a child and which you had now reclaimed after the sale of the house in Stanfordville). Two middle rooms, one without windows, which you

converted into a makeshift study, the other the living room (one window overlooking the garden), followed by the kitchen (one window) and the bathroom in back—tawdry and run-down, yes, but a big step up from where you had been living before. You lost the place on Varick Street in January 1980 (the artist was giving up his loft), and when Manhattan rents proved to be too steep for an apartment that could accommodate both you and your two-and-a-half-year-old son (who spent three days a week with you), you crossed the East River and began searching in Brooklyn. Why hadn't you thought of this in 1976? you wondered. Surely this was a better solution than trekking one hundred miles to the north and buying a haunted house in Dutchess County, but the fact was that Brooklyn had never even crossed your mind back then, for New York was Manhattan and Manhattan only, and the outer boroughs were as alien to you as the distant countries of Oceania or the Arctic Circle. You wound up in Carroll Gardens, a self-enclosed Italian neighborhood where most people went out of their way to make you feel unwelcome, treating you with suspicion and silent stares, as if you were an intruder in their midst, an *estranger,* even if you could have passed for Italian yourself, but no doubt there was something wrong with you, the way you dressed, perhaps, or the way you moved, or simply the look in your eyes. Again and again for almost two years, walking down Carroll Street on the way to your apartment with the old women sitting on the stoops of their houses, cutting off their conversations when you were within earshot of them, watching you pass without a word, and the men standing around with nothing in their eyes, or else looking under the hoods of their cars, examining the engines of those cars with such persistence and dedication that they reminded you of philosophers in search of some ultimate truth about human existence, and the only time you ever received a nod from the women was when you were walking down that street with your son, your little blond-haired son, but otherwise you were a phantom, a man who was not there because he had no business being there. Fortunately, the owners of your building, John and Jackie Caramello, a couple in their early thirties who lived in the garden apartment on the bottom floor, were affable and friendly and never displayed the slightest resentment toward you, but they were your contemporaries, and they were no longer grinding the axes of their parents' generation. Joey Gallo's aunt lived on your block, there were the social clubs around the corner on Henry Street where the old-timers hung out during the day, and if Carroll Gardens was known as the safest neighborhood in the city, it was because it was ruled by an undercurrent of violence, the retaliatory violence and ethics of the mob. Black people steered clear of this well-guarded enclave, knowing they would be risking danger if they set foot within its borders, an unwritten law you might not have understood if you hadn't seen it executed with your own eyes, walking down Court Street one day in the brightness of an autumn afternoon, when a rangy black kid carrying a boom box on the other side of the street was jumped by three or four white teenagers, who pummeled him, bloodied him, and smashed his radio against the sidewalk, and before you could intervene the black kid was staggering away, stumbling forward, and then starting to run as the white kids shouted *nigger* at him and warned him never to come back. Another time, you did have a chance to intervene. A Sunday afternoon in late spring, walking down Carroll Street toward the subway station on Smith, when you stopped for a couple of minutes to watch a roller-skate hockey game being played on the asphalt surface of Carroll Park and saw, hanging on the chain-link fence that surrounded the park, a large red, white, and black Nazi banner. You went into the park, found the sixteen-year-old boy who had put it up (the equipment manager of one of the teams), and told him to take it down. Perplexed, not at all understanding why you would ask him to do such a thing, he listened to you explain what the banner represented, and when he heard you talk about the evils of Hitler and the slaughter of innocent millions, he looked genuinely embarrassed. "I didn't know," he said. "I just thought it looked cool." Rather than ask him where he had been all his life, you waited until he had removed the banner and then continued walking to the subway. Still, Carroll Gardens was not without its advantages, the food in particular, the bakeries, the pork stores, the watermelon man riding through the neighborhood with his horse-drawn wagon in the summer, the coffee roasted on-site at D'Amico's and the blast of sharp, beautiful smells that assaulted you whenever you walked into that shop, but Carroll Gardens was also the place where you asked the single most stupid question of your adult life. You were upstairs in your apartment one afternoon, at work on the second half of *The Invention of Solitude* in your windowless study, when a great clamor of voices rose up from the street outside. You went downstairs to see what was going on, and the whole block was out in force, clusters of men and women were standing in front of their houses, twenty excited conversations were going on at once, and there was your landlord, the burly John Caramello, parked on the stoop of the building where you both lived, calmly surveying the commotion. You asked him what was wrong, and he told you that a man who had just been let out of prison had been breaking into empty houses and apartments along the block and stealing things—jewelry, silverware, anything of value he could put his hands on—but he had been caught before he could get away. That was when you asked your question, uttering the famous words that proved you were an out-and-out dunce who still understood nothing about the little world in which you happened to be living. "Did you call the police?" John smiled. "Of course not," he said. "The boys beat the shit out of him, broke his legs with baseball bats, and threw him into a taxi. He won't be back in this neighborhood again—not if he wants to go on breathing." So much for your early days in Brooklyn, where you have been living for thirty-one years now, and in that transitional period of your life, beginning with the breakup of your marriage and your father's death, the nine months on Varick Street and the first eleven months in Carroll Gardens, a time marked by nightmares and inner struggle, alternating between fits of hope and no hope, tumbling into the beds of various women, women you tried to love and almost loved but couldn't, certain you would never marry again, working on your book, on your translations of Joubert and Mallarmé, on your mammoth anthology of twentieth-century French poetry, taking care of your confused and sometimes embattled three-year-old son, and with so many things happening to you at once, which included the near-fatal cardiac arrest of your mother's second husband just ten days after your father's funeral, the vigils in the hospital six months later as you watched over your grandfather's rapid decline and death, it was probably inevitable that your body should go haywire again, this time with a pounding heart, an irregular heart that would suddenly and inexplicably speed up inside your chest, the bouts of tachycardia that would take hold of you at night just as you were falling asleep, or wake you up just after you had fallen asleep, either alone in the room with your son or lying next to the sleeping bodies of Ann or Françoise or Ruby, the frantically beating heart that would echo inside your head with a percussiveness so loud and insistent you thought the noises were coming from somewhere in the room, a thyroid condition as you eventually found out, which had thrown your system entirely out of whack and for which you had to take pills for two or three years. Then, on February 23, 1981, twenty days after your thirty-fourth birthday, just four days after her twenty-sixth birthday, you met her, you found yourself being introduced to the One, the woman who has been with you ever since that night thirty years ago, your wife, the grand love that ambushed you when you were least expecting it, and in the first weeks you were together, when much of your time was spent in bed, you developed a ritual of reading fairy tales to each other, something you went on doing until your daughter was born six years later, and not long after you discovered the intimate pleasures of reading to each other in this way, your wife wrote a long prose poem entitled *Reading to You,* the fourteenth and last part of which evokes the erratic beating of your heart and is set in the bedroom of your third-floor apartment at 153 Carroll Street: *The cruel father sends the stupid boy into the woods to be killed, but the murderer cannot do it and lets him go, bringing back a deer's heart to the father instead, and this boy speaks to the dogs and the frogs and the birds and in the end the doves whisper into his ears, the words of the mass, the repetitions over and over into his ears, and somewhere else I whisper into your ears, messages, messages from me to you, about the back of your knees and the inside of your elbows and the impression above your upper lip, from me to you even if you are now away. I whisper like the birds in the story I read to you, repetitions in the room where you took me. The parts are the same, but changing, always in movement, altering imperceptibly like the expression on your face from a smile to seriousness leaning over me in the thin light. So I wish you a story in the read-*

ing of it, in the writing of it. We inherit stories, too, conditions, faces, hearts, bladders, weak and stricken. His heart has water around it, drowning, the sick heart, the heart sick, the stricken part, the beat measured in you that is sometimes too fast so you take pills to make it slower, to make it right and rhythmic, not random and slipping like other things. I wish you a story in bed where they hang the moon after the old men die so it shines forever on top of you, and will not stop even if it does not have its own light, but is borrowed and cyclic. I will take the moon, the borrowing and stealing and changing from large to small. The tiniest moon, thin and weak behind a cloud in winter is the view I choose.

19. 18 Tompkins Place; Brooklyn. The top two floors of a four-story brownstone on a one-block street of nearly identical row houses in Cobble Hill, the neighborhood between Carroll Gardens and Brooklyn Heights. Age 34 to 39. Less than half a mile from 153 Carroll Street, but an altogether different world, with a population more mixed and various than the ethnic compound you had lived in for the past twenty-one months. Not a duplex shut off from the lower half of the house but two independent floors, the low-ceilinged one on top with a nook-sized kitchen, an ample dining area and unpartitioned living room beyond it, as well as a small study for your wife; on the higher-ceilinged floor below: a compact master bedroom, a larger bedroom/playroom for your son, and a study for you, identical in size to your wife's above.

A bit ramshackle in overall design, but larger than any apartment you had ever rented and located on a block of great architectural beauty: every house constructed in the 1860s, gas lamps burning at night in front of every door, and when the snow covered the ground in winter, you felt that you had traveled back to the nineteenth century, that if you shut your eyes and listened closely enough, you would hear the sound of horses in the street. You were married in that apartment on a sultry day in mid-June, one of those hot, overcast days in early summer with storms building slowly at the far edge of the horizon, the sky darkening imperceptibly as the hours advanced, and an instant after you were declared man and wife, at the very instant you took your wife in your arms and kissed her, the storm finally broke, a tremendous clap of thunder ripped through the air directly above you, rattling the windows of the house, shaking the floor under your feet, and as the people in the room gasped, it was as if the heavens were announcing your marriage to the world. An uncanny bit of dramatic timing, which meant nothing and yet seemed to mean everything, and for the first time in your life, you felt that you were taking part in a cosmic event.

20. 458 Third Street, Apartment 3R; Brooklyn. A long, narrow apartment that took up one half of the third floor of a four-story building in Park Slope. Living room overlooking the street in front, dining room and galley kitchen in the middle, flanked by a book-lined hallway that led to three small bedrooms in the back. Age 40 to 45. When you moved to your previous apartment on Tompkins Place, your land-

lord, who also happened to be your downstairs neighbor, warned you that you could not live there forever, that eventually he and his family would be taking over the entire house. You must have understood this at the time, but after living there for five years and one month, your longest stint in any dwelling since your boyhood days on Irving Avenue, you had little by little pushed the thought of involuntary departure out of your mind, and because the years on Tompkins Place had been the happiest, most fulfilling period of your life so far, you simply refused to face the facts. Then, in November 1986—just one week after your wife discovered she was pregnant—the landlord politely informed you that time was up and he would not be renewing your lease. His announcement came as a jolt, and because you never wanted to be in such a position again, could not bear the idea of being thrown out of yet another place at some point in the future, you and your wife began searching for a place to buy, a co-op apartment that would belong to you and thereafter protect you from the whims of other people. The Wall Street crash of 1987 was still eleven months off, and the New York real estate frenzy was surging out of control, prices were going up every week, every day, every minute of every day, and because you had only so much money to spend on a down payment, you had to settle for something that did not quite measure up to your needs. The apartment on Third Street was attractive, hands down the most attractive of the many places you had visited on your search, but it was too small for four people, especially when two of the people were writers, who not only had to live in that space but work there as well. All three bedrooms were accounted for: one for you and your wife, one for your son (who continued to live with you half the time), and one for your infant daughter, and even the largest of the three, the so-called master bedroom, was too tightly proportioned to accommodate a desk. Your wife volunteered to set up her work space in a corner of the living room, and you went out and found yourself a tiny studio in an apartment building on Eighth Avenue, a block and a half from 458 Third Street (see entry 20A). Too cramped, then, a less than ideal arrangement, but your circumstances were far from tragic. You and your wife both preferred the animation of Park Slope to the quiet streets of Cobble Hill, and when you started spending the summers in southern Vermont (three months for five consecutive years—see entry 20B), there was little or nothing to complain about, especially when you considered some of the wretched places you had inhabited in the past. Living in a co-op put you in more intimate contact with your neighbors than at any time before or since, something you initially faced with a certain amount of dread, but there were no Madame Rubinsteins in your building, no festering conflicts developed on any front, and the co-op meetings you were obliged to attend were relatively short, easygoing affairs. Six families were involved, four of them with small children, and with an architect, a contractor, and a lawyer among the members of the board, your neighbors were conscientious about maintaining the physical and financial health of the building. Your wife, who served as recording secretary for the five years you lived there, wrote up the minutes after each board meeting—entertaining, tongue-in-cheek reports that were warmly appreciated by everyone involved. Some excerpts:

10/19/87. BUGS: This highly unpleasant subject was addressed by the assembled company with utmost delicacy. The euphemism "problem" was used by at least one member. Marguerite went so far as to speak of "hundreds of babies." Dick recommended a product called COMBAT. Siri echoed the recommendation. It was also suggested that the exterminator be told to change his poison. Then, with a sigh of relief, the members turned to another subject.

3/7/88. THE FENCE: Theo was given a price of $500 for the fence by his students. Certain members felt this was exorbitant; others didn't. There was a faint agreement—that is, an agreement so vague, so slim, it might not be called an agreement at all—that if these students of Theo promised to do a good job, they could have their $500. But this is not certain . . .

10/18/88. OLD BUSINESS: There was a moment of hesitation. Would the members be able to reach into the past and recall just what our old business was? The president came to the rescue with a copy of the old minutes.

2/22/90. CEILING IN 3R: Paul announces to the group that the ceiling in #3R is about to collapse.

Expressions of alarm can be seen on the faces of his fellow co-opers. His wife, otherwise known as the secretary, attempts to assuage the others by noting her husband's tendency to exaggerate. The man's bread and butter, after all, is in the making of fictions, and occasionally this submersion in the world of the imagination colors that other world, known for lack of a better expression as the Real World. Let it stand for the record that the ceiling in 3R is not about to collapse and that its occupants have taken appropriate action to make certain that this will not happen. The plasterers and painters shall take care of our slight sag . . .

3/28/90. CEILING IN 3R: It WAS falling in! The painters who restored that apartment to an acceptable condition confirmed Paul's gloomy prediction. It was just a matter of time before it fell on our heads.

6/17/92. FLOODING: The basement is flooding. Lloyd's acute remark that either we fix the flooding or stock the basement with trout hit home. The estimates for repair are running between $100 and $850, depending on what must be done. We agreed that lower was better than higher and that we should begin low with Roto-Rooter. The gentleman from Roto-Rooter, a friend, acquaintance, or at least a person KNOWN to Lloyd, is Raymond Clean, a name that inspires confidence, considering the nature of his work, and, who knows, may have inspired Mr. Clean's calling in life.

10/15/92. WINDOWS AND CRIME: Joe, the window man, was formally accused of absconding with the secretary's one hundred dollars and not answering his telephone. He may have left the country. Theo and Marguerite have also accused him of essentially NOT FIXING their balances, since they ceased to work again after one week. There was some speculation among the members as to how far one could get with $100. We may have to look for him in Hoboken.

12/3/92. Beyond the walls of 458 Third Street, the weather was cold and damp that night, and winter was upon us. We ended the meeting on a wistful note. Marguerite told stories about Cyprus, a definite longing in her voice. In that exotic place the weather is warm and the light brilliant and clothes dry on balconies in ten minutes. . . . And that is how it stands with us. There's always another place where the sun shines, where clothes dry fast, where there are no window men, no maintenances, no workmen's compensation, or flooded basements . . .

1/14/93. WORKMEN'S COMPENSATION: This issue of whether or not to cover officers of the co-op injured while performing their duties came to a head. We won't. Let come what may: fingers broken at the typewriter, necks strangled in a telephone cord while conducting co-op business, broken legs, arms, and heads from too much wine at a meeting. We'll have to live with it, the way people used to. We'll call it fate. We'll save about fifty bucks, and fifty bucks is fifty bucks is fifty bucks.

20A. 300 Eighth Avenue, Apartment 1-I; Brooklyn. A one-room studio on the ground floor of a six-story apartment building, located in the back, with a view of an air shaft and a brick wall. Larger than the maid's room on the rue du Louvre, less than half the size of the Varick Street hovel, but equipped with a toilet and bath as well as various kitchen appliances built into one of the walls: sink, stove, and mini-bar fridge, which you rarely bothered to use, since this was a space for work and not for living (or eating). A desk, a chair, a metal bookcase, and a couple of storage cabinets; a bare bulb hanging from the middle of the ceiling; an air conditioner in one of the windows, which you would turn on when you arrived in the morning to filter out noises from the building (COOL in summer; FAN in winter). Spartan surroundings, yes, but surroundings have never been of any importance as far as your work is concerned, since the only space you occupy when you write your books is the page in front of your nose, and the room in which you are sitting, the various rooms in which you have sat these forty-plus years, are all but invisible to you as you push your pen across the page of your notebook or transcribe what you have written onto a clean page with your typewriter, the same machine you have been using since your return from France in 1974, an Olympia portable you bought secondhand from a friend for forty dollars—a still functioning relic that was built in a West German factory more than half a century ago and will no doubt go on functioning long after you are dead. The number of your studio apartment pleased you for its symbolic aptness. 1-I, meaning the single self, the lone person sequestered in that bunker of a room for seven or eight hours a day, a silent man cut off from the rest of the world, day after day sitting at his desk for no other purpose than to explore the interior of his own head.

20B. Windham Road; West Townshend, Vermont. A two-story white clapboard house (circa 1800) on the crest of a steep dirt road three miles outside the village of West Townshend. June through August, 1989 through 1993. For the modest sum of one thousand dollars a month, you escaped the tropical heat of New York and the confines of your too-small apartment for this refuge in the hills of southern Vermont. A grassy, quarter-of-an-acre yard in front of the house; dense woods just beyond the yard that stretched on through several miles of wilderness; more woods on the other side of the dirt road; a small pond nearby; an outbuilding at the edge of the yard. Except for a sink and a cheap ancient stove in the kitchen, there were no amenities of any kind: no washing machine, no dishwasher, no television, no bathtub. Telephone communication via party line; radio reception touch and go at best. Freshly painted on the outside, the house was falling apart within: warped floors, buckling ceilings, squadrons of mice in the closets and bureaus, hideous, water-stained wallpaper in the bedrooms, and uncomfortable furniture throughout—lumpy, sagging beds; wobbly chairs; and a cushionless, understuffed couch in the living room. No one lived there anymore. The now-dead former owner, an aged spinster with no immediate heirs, had bequeathed the house to the children of various friends of hers, eight men and women who lived in different parts of the country, from California to Florida, but none in Vermont, none anywhere in New England. They were too scattered and uninvolved to do anything about the house, could not agree on whether to sell it, improve it, or tear it down, and left the oversight of the property to a local real estate agent. The last tenant, a young woman who had turned the place into a marijuana farm and had made a thriving business of it by employing a tough biker gang as her sales force, was now looking at a stiff prison term. After her arrest, the house had remained unoccupied for a couple of years, and when you and your wife rented it in the spring of 1989, on the strength of a single exterior shot of the house (so pretty), you had no idea what you were getting yourselves into. Yes, you had told the agent you were looking for something remote, that *rustic* was a word that did not frighten you or induce any qualms, but even though he'd warned you that the house was not in tip-top condition, neither one of you had imagined you would be walking into a tumbledown shanty. You remember the first night you spent there, wondering out loud if it would be possible to endure an entire summer in such a place, but your wife absorbed the shock more calmly than you did, telling you to be patient, to give it a week or so before you decided to jump ship, that it could turn out to be a lot better than you thought. The next morning, she launched into a furious campaign of scrubbing, bleaching, and disinfecting, opening windows to air out the stuffy rooms, discarding torn curtains and disintegrated blankets, cleaning the blackened stove and oven, removing trash and reorganizing the kitchen cupboards, sweeping, dusting, and polishing, her Scandinavian blood boiling with the righteousness and devotion of her frontier ancestors, while you went across the yard with your notebooks and typewriter to the outbuilding, a cabinlike structure of more recent vintage, which had been trashed by the marijuana girl and her biker friends and turned into a dump site of broken furniture, ripped screen windows, and graffiti-covered walls, a place beyond hope or salvation, and little by little you did what you could to clean up the mess, to get rid of the broken things, to wash the cracked linoleum floors, and within a couple of days you had installed yourself at a green wooden table in the front room and were back to work on your novel, and once you began to settle in, to occupy the house your wife had rescued from filth and disarray, you discovered that you liked being there, that what at first had seemed to be a ubiquitous, unalterable squalor was in fact no more than a state of weary dilapidation, and you could live with crooked floors and ceilings that were falling in, you could learn to ignore the house's defects because it wasn't your house, and little by little you came to appreciate the many advantages the place had to offer: the silence, the coolness of the Vermont air (sweaters in the morning, even on the warmest days), the afternoon strolls through the woods, the sight of your little daughter romping naked through the yard, the tranquil isolation that allowed you and your wife to pursue your work without interference. And so you kept going back, summer after summer, celebrating your daughter's second birthday there, her third birthday, her fourth birthday, her fifth birthday, her sixth birthday, and eventually you began to toy with the idea of buying the house, which wouldn't have cost much, far less than any other house for miles around, but when you considered the expense of restoring your summertime ruin, of rescuing it from imminent collapse and death, you realized that you couldn't afford such an undertaking and that if and when you had the money at your disposal, you should leave your too-small co-op apartment on Third Street and find a larger place to live in New York.

21. Somewhere in Park Slope; Brooklyn. A four-story brownstone with a small garden in back, built in 1892. Age 46 to the present. Your wife left Minnesota in the fall of 1978 to enter the Ph.D. program in English literature at Columbia. She chose Columbia because she wanted to be in New York, had turned down larger, more monumental fellowships from Cornell and Michigan in order to be in New York, and by the time you met her in February 1981, she was a veteran Manhattanite, a committed Manhattanite, a person who

could no longer imagine living anywhere else. Then she threw her lot in with you and wound up settling in the urban hinterlands of Brooklyn. Not unhappily, perhaps, but Brooklyn had never been part of the plan, and now that the two of you had decided to look for another place to live, you told her you were willing to go anywhere she wanted, that you were not so attached to Brooklyn that leaving it would cause you any regrets, and if she wanted to return to Manhattan, you would be happy to start looking with her there. No, she said, without pausing to think about it, without having to think about it, let's stay in Brooklyn. Not only did she not want to go back to Manhattan, she wanted to go on living in the same neighborhood where you were now. Fortunately, the real estate market had collapsed by then, and even though you had to sell your once overpriced apartment at a loss, the house you bought was just within your means—or just beyond them, but not by so much as to cause any lasting difficulties. It took you a year of dogged looking to find it, followed by another six months after the closing before you could move in, but then it was yours, a place finally big enough for all of you, all the bedrooms and studies you needed, all the wall space you needed to shelve the thousands of books you owned, a kitchen large enough to breathe in, bathrooms large enough to breathe in, a guest room for visiting friends and family, a deck off the kitchen for warm-weather drinks and meals, the little garden below, and bit by bit, over the eighteen years you have lived there, which is far longer than you have lived anywhere else, three times longer than your longest run in any other place, you have steadily repaired and improved every inch of every room on every floor, turning a somewhat shabby, down-at-the-heels old house into something sparkling and beautiful, a place that gives you pleasure every time you walk into it, and after eighteen years you are long past the point of thinking about houses in other neighborhoods, other cities, other countries. This is where you live, and this is where you want to go on living until you can no longer walk up and down the stairs. No, even more than that: until you can no longer *crawl* up and down the stairs, until they carry you out and put you in your grave.

Twenty-one permanent addresses from birth to the present, although *permanent* hardly seems to be the right word when you consider how often you have moved during the course of your life. Twenty stopping places, then, a score of addresses leading to the one address that may or may not prove to be permanent, and yet even though you have hung your hat in those twenty-one different houses and apartments, have paid your gas and electric bills there, have been registered to vote there, your body has rarely sat still for any length of time, and when you open a map of your country and begin to count, you discover that you have set foot in forty of the fifty states, sometimes just passing through (as with Nebraska on your train trip to the West Coast in 1976) but more often for visits of several days or weeks or even months, as with Vermont, for example, or California, where you not only lived for half a year but also visited from time to time after your mother and stepfather moved there in the early seventies, not to speak of the twenty-five or twenty-seven trips you have made to Nantucket, the annual summer visits to your friend who owns a house on the island, no less than a week each year, which would tally up to approximately six months total, or the many months you have spent in Minnesota with your wife, the two full summers you lived there when her parents were in Norway, the innumerable spring and winter visits throughout the eighties, nineties, and aughts, perhaps fifty times in all, meaning more than a year of your life, along with frequent trips to Boston starting when you were in your teens, the protracted rambles through the Southwest in 1985 and 1999, the various ports where your tanker docked along the gulf coasts of Texas and Florida when you worked as a merchant seaman in 1970, the visiting-writer jobs that have taken you to such places as Philadelphia, Cincinnati, Ann Arbor, Bowling Green, Durham, and Normal, Illinois, the Amtrak jaunts to Washington, D.C., when you were doing your National Story Project for NPR, the four months of summer camp in New Hampshire when you were eight and ten, the three long sojourns in Maine (1967, 1983, and 1999), and, not to be overlooked, your weekly returns to New Jersey from 1986 to 1990 when you were teaching at Princeton. How many days spent away from home, how many nights spent sleeping in beds that were not your bed? Not just here in America but abroad as well, for when you open your atlas to a map of the world, you see that you have been to all the continents except Africa and Antarctica, and even if you discount the three and a half years you lived in France (where, temporarily, you had several permanent addresses), your visits to foreign countries have been frequent and sometimes rather long: an additional year in France on numerous other trips both before and after the time you lived there, five months in Portugal (most of them in 2006, for the shooting of your last film), four months in the U.K. (England, Scotland, and Wales), three months in Canada, three months in Italy, two months in Spain, two months in Ireland, a month and a half in Germany, a month and a half in Mexico, a month and a half on the island of Bequia (in the Grenadines), a month in Norway, a month in Israel, three weeks in Japan, two and a half weeks in Holland, two weeks in Denmark, two weeks in Sweden, two weeks in Australia, nine days in Brazil, eight days in Argentina, one week on the island of Guadeloupe, one week in Belgium, six days in the Czech Republic, five days in Iceland, four days in Poland, and two days in Austria. You would like to tote up how many hours you have spent traveling to these places (that is, how many days, weeks, or months), but you wouldn't know how to begin, you have lost track of how many trips you have made in America, have no idea how often you have left America and gone abroad, and therefore you could never come up with an exact or even approximate number to tell you how many thousands of hours of your life have been spent in between places, going from here to there and back, the mountains of time you have given over to sitting in airplanes, buses, trains, and cars, the time squandered fighting to overcome the effects of jet lag, the boredom of waiting for your flight to be announced in airports, the deadly tedium of standing around the luggage carousel as you wait for your bag to tumble down the chute, but nothing is more disconcerting to you than the ride in the plane itself, the strange sense of being nowhere that engulfs you each time you step into the cabin, the unreality of being propelled through space at five hundred miles an hour, so far off the ground that you begin to lose a sense of your own reality, as if the fact of your own existence were slowly being drained out of you, but such is the price you pay for leaving home, and as long as you continue to travel, the nowhere that lies between the here of home and the there of somewhere else will continue to be one of the places where you live.

You would like to know who you are. With little or nothing to guide you, you take it for granted that you are the product of vast, prehistoric migrations, of conquests, rapes, and abductions, that the long and circuitous intersections of your ancestral horde have extended over many territories and kingdoms, for you are not the only person who has traveled, after all, tribes of human beings have been moving around the earth for tens of thousands of years, and who knows who begat whom begat whom begat whom begat whom begat whom to end up with your two parents begetting you in 1947? You can go back only as far as your grandparents, with some scant information about your great-grandparents on your mother's side, which means that the generations that came before them are no more than blank space, a void of conjecture and blind guesswork. All four of the grandparents were Eastern European Jews, the two on your father's side born in the late 1870s in the city of Stanislav in the backwater province of Galicia, then part of the Austro-Hungarian Empire, subsequently part of Poland after World War I, later part of the Soviet Union after World War II, and now part of Ukraine following the end of the Cold War, whereas the two on your mother's side were born in 1893 and 1895, your grandmother in Minsk and your grandfather in Toronto—a year after his family emigrated from Warsaw. Both of your grandmothers were redheads, and on both sides of your family there is a tumultuous mix of physical features in the many offspring who followed them, ranging from the dark-haired to the blond, from the brown-skinned to the pale and freckled, from curls and waves to no curls and no waves, from stout peasant bodies with thick legs and stubby fingers to the lithe and elongated contours of still other bodies. The Eastern European genetic pool, but who knows where those nameless ghosts had been wandering before they came to the cities of Russia, Poland, and the Austro-Hungarian Empire, for how else to account for the fact that your sister was born with a Mongolian blue spot on her back, something that occurs only in Asian babies, and how else to account for the fact that you, with your brownish skin and wavy hair and gray-green eyes, have eluded ethnic identification for your entire life and have been variously told by strangers that you must be and most certainly are an Italian, a Greek, a Spaniard, a Lebanese, an Egyptian, and even a Pakistani? Because you know nothing about where you come from, you long ago decided to presume that you are a composite of all the races of the Eastern Hemisphere, part African, part Arab, part Chinese, part Indian, part Caucasian, the melting pot of numerous warring civilizations in a single body. As much as anything else, it is a moral position, a way of eliminating the question of race, which is a bogus question in your opinion, a question that can only bring dishonor to the person who asks it, and therefore you have consciously decided to be everyone, to embrace everyone inside you in order to be most fully and freely yourself, since who you are is a mystery and you have no hope that it will ever be solved.

Your birthday has come and gone. Sixty-four years old now, inching ever closer to senior citizenship, to the days of Medicare and Social Security benefits, to a time when more and more of your friends will have left you. So many of them are gone already—but just wait for the deluge that is coming. Much to your relief, the event passed without incident or commotion, you calmly took it in your stride, a small dinner with friends in Brooklyn, and the impossible age you have now reached seldom entered your thoughts. February third, just one day after your mother's birthday, who went into labor with you on the morning she turned twenty-two, nineteen days before it was supposed to happen, and when the doctor pulled you out of her drugged body with a pair of forceps, it was twenty minutes past midnight, less than half an hour after her birthday had ended. You therefore always celebrated your birthdays together, and even now, almost nine years after her death, you inevitably think about her whenever the clock turns from the second of February to the third. What an unlikely present you must have been that night sixty-four years ago: a baby boy for her birthday, a birth to celebrate her birth.

May 2002. On Saturday, the long, highly spirited conversation with your mother on the telephone, at the end of which you turn to your wife and say: "She hasn't sounded this happy in years." On Sunday, your wife leaves for Minnesota. A large celebration for her father's eightieth birthday has been planned for next weekend, and she is going to Northfield in order to help her mother with the arrangements. You stay behind in New York with your daughter, who is fourteen and must attend school, but the two of you will of course be traveling to Minnesota for the party as well, and your tickets have been booked for Friday. In anticipation of the event, you have already written a humorous rhyming poem in your father-in-law's honor—which is the only kind of poem you write anymore: frivolous bagatelles for birthdays, weddings, and other family occasions. Monday comes and goes, and everything that happened that day has been obliterated from your memory. On Tuesday, you have a one o'clock meeting with a Frenchwoman in her mid-twenties who has been living in New York for the past several years. She has been engaged by a French publisher to write a guidebook of the city, and because you like this person and feel she is a promising writer, you have agreed to talk to her about New York, doubtful that anything you say will be of much use to her project, but nevertheless you are willing to give it a try. At noon, you are standing in front of the bathroom mirror with shaving cream on your face, about to pick up the razor and begin the job of making yourself presentable for the interview, but before you can attack a single whisker, the telephone rings. You go into the bedroom to answer it, awkwardly positioning the receiver in your hand so as not to cover it with shaving cream, and the voice on the other end is sobbing, the person who has called you is in a state of extreme distress, and little by little you understand that it is Debbie, the young woman who cleans your mother's apartment once a week and occasionally drives her on errands, and what Debbie is telling you now is that she just let herself into the apartment and found your mother on the bed, your mother's body on the bed, your dead mother's body on the bed. Your insides seem to empty out as you take in the news. You feel dazed and hollow, unable to think, and even if this is the last thing you were expecting to happen now (*She hasn't sounded this happy in years*), you are not surprised by what Debbie is telling you, not stunned, not shocked, not even upset. What is wrong with you? you ask yourself. Your mother has just died, and you've turned into a block of wood. You tell Debbie to wait where she is, you will get there as quickly as you can (Verona, New Jersey—next to Montclair), and an hour and a half later you are in your mother's apartment, looking at her corpse on the bed. You have seen several corpses in the past, and you are familiar with the inertness of the dead, the inhuman stillness that envelops the bodies of the no longer living, but none of those corpses belonged to your mother, no other dead body was the body in which your own life began, and you can look for no more than a few seconds before you turn your head away. The blue-tinged pallor of her skin, her half-closed eyes fixed on nothing, an extinguished self lying on top of the covers in her nightgown and bathrobe, the Sunday paper sprawled around her, one bare leg dangling over the edge of the bed, a spot of white drool hardened in a corner of her mouth. You cannot look at her, you will not look at her, you find it unbearable to look at her, and yet even after the paramedics have wheeled her out of the apartment in a black body bag, you continue to feel nothing. No tears, no howls of anguish, no grief—just a vague sense of horror growing inside you. Your cousin Regina is with you now, your mother's first cousin, who has driven over from her house in nearby Glen Ridge to lend you a hand, the daughter of your grandfather's only brother, five or six years younger than your mother, your first cousin once removed and one of the few people on either side of your family you feel any connection to, an artist, widow of another artist, the young bohemian woman who fled Brooklyn in the early fifties to live in the Village, and she stays with you throughout the day, she and her grown daughter Anna, the two of them helping you sort through your mother's belongings and papers, conferring with you as you struggle to decide what to do about someone who left no will and never talked about her wishes after death (burial or cremation, funeral or no funeral), making lists with you of all the practical tasks that must be dealt with sooner rather than later, and that evening, after dinner in a restaurant, they take you back to their house and show you the guest room where you can spend the night. Your daughter is staying with friends in Park Slope, your wife is with her parents in Minnesota, and after a long talk with her on the phone after dinner, you are unable to sleep. You have bought a bottle of scotch to keep you company, and so you sit in a downstairs room until three or four in the morning, consuming half the bottle of Oban as you try to think about your mother, but your mind is still too numb to think about much of anything. Scattered thoughts, inconsequential thoughts, and still no impulse to cry, to break down and mourn your mother with an earnest display of sorrow and regret. Perhaps you are afraid of what will happen to you if you let yourself go, that once you allow yourself to cry you will not be able to stop yourself, that the pain will be too crushing and you will fall to pieces, and because you don't want to risk losing control of yourself, you hold on to the pain, swallow it, bury it in your heart. You miss your wife, miss her more than at any time since you have been married, for she is the only person who knows you well enough to ask the right questions, who has the assurance and understanding to prod you into revealing things about yourself that often elude your own understanding, and how much better it would be if you were lying in bed with her now instead of sitting alone in a darkened room at three in the morning with a bottle of whiskey. The next morning, your cousins continue to prop you up and help you with the tasks at hand, the visit to the mortuary and the selection of an urn (after consulting with your wife, your mother's sister, and your cousin, the unanimous decision was cremation and no funeral, with a memorial service to be held sometime after the summer), the calls to the real estate man, the car man, the furniture man, the cable television man, all the men you must contact in order to sell, disconnect, and discard, and then, after a long day submerged in the bleak miasma of *nothing*, they drive you back to your house in Brooklyn. You all share a takeout dinner with your daughter, you thank Regina for having *saved your life* (your exact words, since you truly don't know what you would have done without her), and once they have left, you stay up for a while talking to your daughter, but eventually she marches upstairs to go to bed, and now that you are alone again, you again find yourself resisting the lure of sleep. The second night is a repetition of the first: sitting alone in a darkened room with the same bottle of scotch, which you drain to the bottom this time, and still no tears, no cogent thoughts, and no inclination to call it a night and turn in. After many hours, exhaustion finally overwhelms you, and when you fall into bed at five-thirty, dawn is already breaking outside and the birds have begun to sing. You plan to sleep for as long as possible, ten or twelve hours if you can manage it, knowing that oblivion is the only cure for you now, but just after eight o'clock, when you have been sleeping for roughly two and a half hours, and sleeping in a way that only the drunk can sleep—*profondamente, stupidamente*—the telephone rings. If the phone were on the other side of the room, it is doubtful you would even hear it, but there it is on the nightstand next to your pillow, not twelve inches from your head, eleven inches from your right ear, and after how many rings (you will never know how many), your eyes involuntarily open. During those first seconds of semiconsciousness, you understand that you have never felt worse, that your body is no longer the body you are used to calling your own, that this new and alien physical self has been hammered by a hundred wooden mallets, dragged by horses for a hundred miles over a barren terrain of rocks and cacti, reduced to a heap of dust by a hundred-ton pile driver. Your bloodstream is so saturated with alcohol that you can smell it coming out of your pores, and the entire room stinks of bad breath and whiskey—fetid, noxious, disgusting. If you want anything now, if one wish could be granted to you, even at the cost of giving up ten years of your life in exchange, it is simply to shut your eyes again and go back to sleep. And yet, for reasons you will never understand (force of habit? a sense of duty? a conviction that the caller is your wife?), you roll over, extend your arm, and pick up the phone. It is one of your cousins, a female first cousin from your father's side of the family, ten years older than you are and a contentious, self-appointed moral judge, the last person on earth you want to talk to, but now that you have picked up the phone, you can't very well hang up on her, not when she is talking, talking, talking, scarcely pausing long enough to let you say a word, to give you a chance to break in and cut the conversation short. How is it possible, you wonder, for someone to rattle on as quickly as she does? It is as if she has trained herself not to breathe while she talks, to spew forth entire paragraphs in a single, uninterrupted exhale, long outrushes of verbiage with no punctuation and no need to stop for an occasional intake of air. Her lungs must be enormous, you think, the largest lungs in the world, and such stamina, such a burning compulsion to have the last word on every subject. You and this cousin have had numerous battles in the past, beginning with the publication of *The Invention of Solitude* in 1982, which in her eyes constituted a betrayal of Auster family secrets (your grandmother murdered your grandfather in 1919), and henceforth you were turned into an outcast, just as your mother was turned into an outcast after she and your father divorced (which is why you have decided against a funeral for her—in order to avoid having to invite certain members of that clan to the service), but at the same time this cousin is not a stupid woman, she is a summa cum laude college graduate, a psychologist with a large and successful practice, an expansive, energetic person who always makes a point of telling you how many of her friends read your novels, and it is true that she has made some efforts to patch things up between you over the years, to nullify the damage of her vicious outburst against your book two decades ago, but even if she professes to admire you now, there is nevertheless an abiding rancor in her as well, an animosity that continues to lurk inside her overtures of friendship, none of it is purely one thing or the other, and the whole situation between you is fraught with complications, for her health is not good, she has been undergoing cancer treatments for some time and you can't help feeling sorry for her, and because she has taken the trouble to call, you want to give her the benefit of the doubt, to allow her this short, perfunctory conversation and then roll over and go back to sleep. She begins by saying all the appropriate things. How sudden, how unexpected, how unprepared you must have been, and think of your sister, your poor schizophrenic sister, how will she cope now that your mother is gone? That is enough, you feel, more than enough to demonstrate her goodwill and sympathy, and you hope you will be able to hang up after another sentence or two, since your eyes are closing now, you are absolutely miserable with exhaustion, and if she would only stop talking within the next few seconds, you would have no trouble drifting off again into the deepest of slumbers. But your cousin is just getting started, rolling up her sleeves and spitting into her hands, as it were, and for the next five minutes she shares her earliest memories of your mother with you, meeting her as a girl of nine when your mother was still so young herself, just twenty or twenty-one, and how thrilling it was to have such a pretty new aunt in the family, so warm and full of life, and so you go on listening, you don't have the strength to interrupt her, and before long she is on another subject altogether, you don't know how she got there, but suddenly you hear her voice talking to you about your smoking, imploring you to stop, to give it up for good, or else you will become sick and die, die a horrendous early death, and as you die you will be filled with remorse for having *murdered yourself* in such a thoughtless way. She has been at it for nine or ten minutes at this point, and you are beginning to worry that you will not be able to go back to sleep, for the longer she goes on, the more you feel yourself being pulled toward consciousness, and once the line is crossed, there will be no turning back. You can't survive on two and a half hours' sleep, not in your present condition, not with so much alcohol still in your blood, you will be destroyed for the whole day, but even though you are feeling more and more tempted to hang up on her, you cannot find the will to do it. Then comes the onslaught, the barrage of verbal cannon fire you should have been expecting from the instant you picked up the phone. How could you have been so naïve as to think that kind words and quasi-hysterical warnings would be the end of it? There is still the question of your mother's character to be dealt with, and even if her body was discovered only two days ago, even if the crematorium in New Jersey has scheduled her body to be burned into ashes this very afternoon, that doesn't prevent your cousin from letting her have it. Thirty-eight years after she left your father, the family has codified its litany of complaints against your mother, it is the stuff of ancestral history by now, old gossip turned into solid facts, and why not go through the list of her misdeeds one last time—in order to give her a proper send-off to the place where she deserves to go? Never satisfied, your cousin says, always looking for something else, too flirtatious for her own good, a woman who lived and breathed to attract the attentions of men, oversexed, whorish, someone who slept around, an unfaithful wife—too bad that a person with so many other good qualities should have been such a mess. You always suspected your mother's ex-in-laws talked about her in that way, but until this morning you have never heard it with your own ears. You mumble something into the telephone and hang up, vowing never to talk to your cousin again, never to utter a single word to her for the rest of your life. Sleep is out of the question now. In spite of the supernatural exhaustion that has clobbered you into near senselessness, too much has been churned up inside you, your thoughts are sprinting off in myriad directions, adrenaline is surging through your system again, and your eyes refuse to close. There is nothing for it but to get out of bed and begin the day. You go downstairs and prepare a pot of coffee, the strongest, blackest coffee you have made in years, figuring that if you flood yourself with titanic doses of caffeine, you will be lifted into something that resembles wakefulness, a partial wakefulness, which will allow you to sleepwalk through the rest of the morning and on into the afternoon. You drink the first cup slowly. It is exceedingly hot and must be swallowed in small sips, but then the coffee begins to cool down, and you drink the second cup more rapidly than the first, the third more rapidly than the second, and swallow by swallow the liquid splashes into your empty stomach like acid. You can feel the caffeine accelerating your heart rate, agitating your nerves, and beginning to light you up. You are awake now, fully awake and yet still weary, drained but ever more alert, and in your head there is a buzzing that wasn't there before, a low-pitched mechanical sound, a humming, a whining, as if from a distant, out-of-tune radio, and the more you drink, the more you feel your body changing, the less you feel that you are made of flesh and blood. You are turning into something metallic now, a rusty contraption that simulates human life, a thing put together with wires and fuses, vast circuits of wires controlled by random electrical impulses, and now that you have finished the third cup of coffee, you pour yourself another—which turns out to be the last one, the lethal one. The attack begins simultaneously from the inside and the outside, a sudden feeling of pressure from the air around you, as if an invisible force were trying to push you through the chair and knock you to the ground, but at the same time an unearthly lightness in your head, a vertiginous jangle thrumming against the walls of your skull, and all the while the outside continues to press in on you, even as the inside grows empty, ever more dark and empty, as if you are about to pass out. Then your pulse quickens, you can feel your heart trying to burst through your chest, and a moment after that there is no more air in your lungs, you can no longer breathe. That is when the panic overwhelms you, when your body shuts down and you fall to the floor. Lying on your back, you feel the blood stop flowing in your veins, and little by little your limbs turn to cement. That is when you start to howl. You are made of stone now, and as you lie there on the dining room floor, rigid, your mouth open, unable to move or think, you howl in terror as you wait for your body to drown in the deep black waters of death.

You couldn't cry. You couldn't grieve in the way people normally do, and so your body broke down and did the grieving for you. If not for the various incidental factors that preceded the onset of panic (your wife's absence, the alcohol, the lack of sleep, your cousin's phone call, the coffee), it is possible the attack never would have taken place. But in the end those elements are of only secondary importance. The question is why you couldn't let yourself go in the minutes and hours that followed your mother's death, why, for two full days, you were unable to shed any tears for her. Was it because a part of you was secretly glad she was dead? A dark thought, a thought so dark and disturbing that it scares you even to express it, but even if you are willing to entertain the possibility that it is true, you doubt that it would account for your failure to cry. You didn't cry after your father's death either. Nor after the deaths of your grandparents, nor after the death of your most beloved cousin, who died of breast cancer when she was thirty-eight, nor after the deaths of the many friends who have left you over the years. Not even at fourteen, when you were less than a foot away from a boy who was struck and killed by lightning, the boy whose dead body you sat next to and watched over for the next hour in a rain-drenched meadow, desperately trying to warm up his body and revive him because you didn't understand he was dead—not even that monstrous death could coax a single tear from you. Your eyes water up when you watch certain movies, you have dropped tears onto the pages of numerous books, you have cried at moments of immense personal sorrow, but death freezes you and shuts you down, robbing you of all emotion, all affect, all connection to your own heart. From the very beginning, you have gone dead in the face of death, and that is what happened to you with your mother's death as well. At least for the first little while, the first two days and nights, but then lightning struck again, and you were scorched.

Forget what your cousin said to you on the phone. You were angry at her, yes, appalled that she would stoop to slinging mud at such an inappropriate time, revolted by her nastiness, her sanctimonious contempt for a person who never did her an ounce of harm, but her accusations of infidelity against your mother were old business to you by then, and even if you had no proof, no evidence to support or deny the charges, you had long suspected that your mother *might* have strayed during her marriage to your father. You were fifty-five years old when you had that conversation with your cousin, and with so much time to have pondered the details of your parents' unfortunate marriage, you in fact hoped that your mother had found some comfort with another man (or men). But nothing was certain, and only once did you have any inkling that something might be amiss, a single moment when you were twelve or thirteen, which thoroughly perplexed you at the time: walking into the house one day after school, thinking no one else was there, picking up the telephone to make a call, and hearing a man's voice on the line, a voice that did not belong to your father, saying no more than *Good-bye*, an altogether neutral word perhaps, but spoken with great tenderness, and then your mother saying back to him, *Good-bye, darling*. That was the end of the conversation. You had no idea what the context was, could not identify the man, had heard almost nothing, and yet you worried about it for days, so much so that you finally found the courage to ask your mother about it, she who had always been honest and direct with you, you felt, who had never refused to answer your questions, but this time, this one time, she looked puzzled when you told her what you had heard, as if she had been caught off guard, and then a moment later she laughed, saying she couldn't remember, she didn't know what you were talking about. It was entirely possible that she didn't remember, that the conversation was of no importance and the endearment had not meant what you thought it had, but a tiny germ of doubt was planted in your head that day, doubt that quickly vanished in the weeks and months that followed, but four or five years later, when your mother announced that she was leaving your father, you couldn't help thinking back to the last sentences of that accidentally overheard conversation. Did any of it matter? No, not that you could think of. Your parents had been destined to split up from the day they were married, and whether your mother had slept with the man she called *darling*, whether there was another man or several men or no man at all, did not play a part in their divorce. Symptoms are not causes, and whatever ugly little thoughts your cousin might have harbored against your mother, she knew nothing about anything. It is undeniable that her call helped to unleash your panic attack—the timing of the call, the circumstances of the call—but what she said to you that morning was stale news.

On the other hand, even though you happened to be her son, you know next to nothing yourself. Too many gaps, too many silences and evasions, too many threads lost over the years for you to stitch together a coherent story. Useless to talk about her from the outside, then. Whatever can be told must be pulled from the inside, from your insides, the accumulation of memories and perceptions you continue to carry around in your body—and which left you, for reasons that will never be entirely known, gasping for breath on the dining room floor, certain you were about to die.

A hasty, ill-considered marriage, an impetuous marriage between two incompatible souls that ran out of steam before the honeymoon was over. A twenty-one-year-old girl from New York (born and bred in Brooklyn, translated to Manhattan at sixteen) and a thirty-four-year-old bachelor from Newark who had begun life in Wisconsin and had left there, fatherless, at the age of seven, when your grandmother shot and killed your grandfather in the kitchen of their house. The bride was the younger of two daughters, the product of yet another ill-considered, mismatched marriage (*Your father would be such a wonderful man—if only he were different*) who had dropped out of high school to work (clerical jobs in offices, later a photographer's assistant) and never told you much about her earlier loves and romances. A vague story about a boyfriend who had died in the war, an even vaguer story about a brief flirtation with actor Steve Cochran, but beyond that nothing at all. She finished up her diploma by going to school at night (Commercial High), but no college afterward, and no college for your father either, who was still a boy when he entered the Land of Work and began supporting himself as soon as he graduated from high school at eighteen. Those are the known facts, the few bits of verifiable information that have been passed down to you. Then come the invisible years, the first three or four years of your life, the blank time before any possibility of recall, and therefore you have nothing to go on but the various stories your mother told you later: your near death at sixteen months from tonsillitis (106° fever, and the doctor telling her: *It's in God's hands now*), the vagaries of your cranky, disobedient stomach, a condition that was diagnosed as an allergy or intolerance to something (wheat? gluten?) and forced you to subsist for two and a half years on a diet limited almost exclusively to bananas (so many bananas consumed in that time before memory that you still recoil from the sight and smell of them and have not eaten one in sixty years), the jutting nail that tore apart your cheek in the Newark department store in 1950, your remarkable ability at age three to identify the make and model of every car on the road (remarkable to your mother, who read it as a sign of incipient genius), but most of all the pleasure she communicated to you in the telling of these stories, the way she seemed to exult in the mere fact of your existence, and because her marriage was such an unhappy one, you realize now that she turned to you as a form of consolation, to give her life a meaning and a purpose it was otherwise lacking. You were the beneficiary of her unhappiness, and you were well loved, especially well loved, without question deeply loved. That first of all, that above and beyond everything else there might be to say: she was an ardent and dedicated mother to you during your infancy and early childhood, and whatever is good in you now, whatever strengths you might possess, come from that time before you can remember who you were.

Some early glimmers, a few small islands of recollection in an otherwise endless sea of black. Waiting for your newborn sister to come home from the hospital with your parents (age: three years and nine months), looking through the slats of the venetian blinds in the living room with your mother's mother and leaping up and down when the car finally stopped in front of the house. According to your mother, you were an enthusiastic older brother, not at all envious of the new baby who had entered your midst, but she seems to have handled the matter with great intelligence, not shutting you out but turning you into her *helper*, which gave you the illusion that you were actively participating in your sister's care. Some months later, you were asked if you wanted to give nursery school a try. You said yes, not quite sure what nursery school was, since preschools were far less common in 1951 than they are now, but after one day you had had enough. You remember having to line up with a group of other children and pretend you were in a grocery store, and when your turn finally came, after what seemed to have been hours, you handed a pile of pretend money to someone standing behind a pretend cash register, who gave you a bag of pretend food in return. You told your mother that nursery school was an idiotic waste of time, and she didn't try to talk you into going back. Then your family moved to the house on Irving Avenue, and when you started kindergarten the following September, you were ready for school, not the least bit fazed by the prospect of spending time away from your mother. You remember the chaotic prelude to the first morning, the children who ranted and screamed when their mothers said good-bye to them, the anguished cries of the abandoned echoing off the walls as you calmly waved good-bye to your own mother, and all that fuss was incomprehensible to you, since you were happy to be there and felt like a big person now. You were five years old, and already you were pulling away, no longer living exclusively in your mother's orbit. Better health, new friends, the freedom of the yard behind the house, and the beginnings of an autonomous life. You still wet the bed, of course, you still cried when you fell down and cut your knee, but the inner dialogue had begun, and you had crossed into the domain of conscious selfhood. Nevertheless, because of the hours he put in at work, and because of his penchant for taking long naps whenever he was at home, your father was largely absent from the household, and your mother continued to be the central force of authority and wisdom for all things that counted most. She was the one who put you to bed, the one who taught you how to ride a bicycle, the one who helped you with your piano lessons, the one you unburdened yourself to, the rock you clung to whenever the seas grew rough. But you were developing a mind of your own, and you were no longer in thrall to her every pronouncement and opinion. You hated practicing the piano, you wanted to be outside playing with your friends, and when you told her that you would prefer to quit, that baseball was vastly more important to you than music, she relented without putting up much of an argument. Then there was the issue of clothes. You mostly ran around in a T-shirt and a pair of jeans (called dungarees back then), but for special occasions—holidays, birthday parties, the visits to your grandparents in New York—she insisted on dressing you in finely tailored outfits, clothes that began to embarrass you by the time you reached six, especially the white-shirt-and-short-pants combo with the knee socks and sandals, and when you began to protest, claiming that you felt ridiculous in those things, that all you wanted was to look like every other American boy, she eventually gave ground and allowed you to have a say in what you wore. But she was pulling away by then, too, and not long after you turned six, she went off to the Land of Work, and you began seeing less and less of her. You don't remember feeling sad about it, but then again, what do you really know about what you felt? The important thing to keep in mind is that you know next to nothing—and nothing whatsoever about the state of her marriage, the depth of her unhappiness with your father. Years later, she told you that she tried to talk him into moving to California, that she felt there would be no hope for them unless he got away from his family, the suffocating presence of his mother and older brothers, and when he refused to consider it, she resigned herself to a marriage of no hope. The children were too small for her to contemplate divorce (not then, not there, not in middle-class America of the early fifties), and so she found another solution. She was only twenty-eight years old, and work opened the door, let her out of the house, and gave her a chance to build a life of her own.

You don't mean to suggest that she disappeared. She was simply less present than before, far less present, and if most of your memories from that period are confined to the little world of your boyhood pursuits (running around with your friends, riding your bicycle, going to school, playing sports, collecting stamps and baseball cards, reading comic books), your mother appears vividly in several instances, particularly when you were eight and for some reason joined the Cub Scouts with a dozen or so of your friends. You can't remember how often the meetings were held, but you suspect it was once a month, each time in the house of a different member, and these gatherings were run by a rotating squad of three or four women, the so-called den mothers, one of whom was your own mother, which proves that her work as a real estate broker was not so crushing that she couldn't afford to take an occasional afternoon off. You remember how much you enjoyed seeing her in her navy blue den mother's uniform (the absurdity of it, the novelty of it), and you also remember that she was the den mother the boys liked best, for she was the youngest and prettiest of all the mothers, the most entertaining, the most relaxed, the one who had no trouble commanding their complete attention. You can recall two of the meetings she ran with utmost clarity: working on the construction of wooden storage boxes (for what purpose you can no longer say, but everyone applied himself to the task with great diligence), and then, toward the end of the school year, when the weather was warm and the entire gang had grown bored with the rules and regulations of scouthood, there was a last or next-to-last meeting at your house on Irving Avenue, and because no one had the stomach for pretending to act like miniature soldiers anymore, your mother asked the boys how they would like to spend the afternoon, and when the unanimous response was *play baseball,* you all went out into the backyard and picked up sides for a game. Because there were only ten or twelve of you and the teams were shorthanded, your mother decided to play as well. You were immensely pleased, but since you had never seen her swing a bat, you weren't expecting her to do much of anything but strike out. When she came up in the second inning and smacked a ball far over the left fielder's head, you were more than pleased, you were flabbergasted. You can still see your mother running around the bases in her den mother's uniform and coming in to the plate with her home run—out of breath, smiling, soaking up the cheers from the boys. Of all the memories you have retained of her from your childhood, this is the one that comes back to you most often.

She probably wasn't beautiful, not beautiful in the classic sense of the term, but pretty enough, more than attractive enough to make men stare at her whenever she walked into a room. What she lacked in the way of pure good looks, the movie-star looks of certain women who may or may not be movie stars, she made up for by exuding an aura of glamour, especially when she was young, from her late twenties to her early forties, a mysterious combination of carriage, poise, and elegance, the clothes that pointed to but did not overstate the sensuality of the person inside them, the perfume, the makeup, the jewelry, the stylishly coiffed hair, and, above all, the playful look in the eyes, at once forthright and demure, *a look of confidence,* and even if she wasn't the most beautiful woman in the world, she acted as if she were, and a woman who can pull that off will inevitably make heads turn, which was no doubt what caused the dour matrons of your father's family to despise her after she left the fold. Those were difficult years, of course, the stretch of years before the long-deferred but inevitable breakup with your father, the years of *Good-bye, darling* and the car she wrecked one night when you were ten. You can still see her bloodied, banged-up face as she walked into the house early the next morning, and although she never told you much about the accident, only a bland, generic account that must have had little to do with the truth, you suspect that alcohol might have been involved, that there was a short period back then when she was drinking too much, for later on she dropped some hints about having been in A.A., and the fact was that she never drank any alcohol for the rest of her life—not one cocktail or glass of champagne, nothing, not even a sip of beer.

There were three of her, three separate women who seemed unconnected to one another, and as you grew older and began to look at her differently, to see her as someone who was not just your mother, you never knew which mask she would be wearing on any given day. At one end, there was the diva, the sumptuously decked-out charmer who dazzled the world in public, the young woman with the obtuse, distracted husband who craved having the eyes of others upon her and would not allow herself—not anymore—to be boxed into the role of traditional housewife. In the middle, which was far and away the largest space she occupied, there was a solid and responsible being, a person of intelligence and compassion, the woman who took care of you when you were young, the woman who went out to work, who ran several small businesses over the course of many years, the four-star joke teller and crossword-puzzle ace, a person with her feet firmly planted on the ground—competent, generous, observant of the world around her, a devoted liberal in her politics, a sage dispenser of advice. At the other end, the extreme end of who she was, there was the frightened and debilitated neurotic, the helpless creature prey to blistering assaults of anxiety, the phobic whose incapacities grew as the years advanced—from an early fear of heights to a metastatic flowering of multiple forms of paralysis: afraid of escalators, afraid of airplanes, afraid of elevators, afraid to drive a car, afraid of going near windows on the upper floors of buildings, afraid to be alone, afraid of open spaces, afraid to walk anywhere (she felt she would lose her balance or pass out), and an ever-present hypochondria that gradually reached the most exalted summits of dread. In other words: afraid to die, which in the end is probably no different from saying: afraid to live. When you were young, you were not aware of any of this. She seemed perfect to you, and even during her first attack of vertigo, which you happened to witness when you were six (the two of you climbing up the inner staircase of the Statue of Liberty), you were not alarmed, because she was a good and conscientious mother, and she managed to hide her fear from you by turning the descent into a game: sitting on the stairs together and going down one step at a time, asses on the rungs, laughing all the way to the bottom. When she was old, there was no more laughter. Only the void spinning around in her head, the knot in her belly, the cold sweats, a pair of invisible hands tightening around her throat.

Her second marriage was a grand success, the marriage everyone longs for—until it wasn't. You were glad to see her so happy, so clearly in love, and you took to her new husband without hesitation, not only because he was in love with your mother and knew how to love her in all the ways you felt she needed to be loved, but because he was an impressive man in his own right, a labor lawyer with an acute mind and a large personality, someone who seemed to take life by storm, who boomed out old standards at the dinner table and told hilarious stories about his past, who instantly embraced you not as a stepson but as a kind of younger brother, which turned you into close, steadfast friends, and all in all you thought this marriage was the best thing that had ever happened to your mother, the thing that would make everything right for her at last. She was still young, after all, still not forty years old, and because he was two years younger than she was, you had every reason to expect they would have a long life together and die in each other's arms. But your stepfather's health was not good. Strong and vigorous as he seemed, he had been cursed with a bad heart, and after a first coronary in his early thirties, he had his second big attack about a year into the marriage, and from then on there was an element of foreboding that hung over their life together, which only worsened when he suffered a third attack a couple of years later. Your mother lived in constant fear of losing him, and you saw with your own eyes how those fears gradually unhinged her, little by little exacerbating the weaknesses she had struggled for so long to keep hidden, the phobic self that roared into full bloom during their last years together, and when he died at fifty-four, she was no longer the person she had been when they were married. You remember her last heroic stand, the night in Palo Alto, California, when she told jokes nonstop to you and your wife as your stepfather lay in the intensive care unit of the Stanford Medical Center undergoing experimental cardiac treatments. The final, desperate move in a case that had been deemed all but hopeless, and the gruesome sight of your mortally ill stepfather lying in that bed hooked up to so many wires and machines that the room looked like the set from a science fiction film, and when you walked in and saw him there, you were so stunned and miserable that you found yourself fighting back tears. It was the summer of 1981, and you and your wife had known each other for about six months, you were living together but not yet married, and as the two of you stood at your stepfather's bedside, he reached out, took hold of both your hands, and said: "Don't waste any time. Get married now. Get married, take care of each other, and have twelve children." You and your wife were staying with your mother in a house somewhere in Palo Alto, an empty house that had been lent to her by some unknown friend, and that night, after eating dinner in a restaurant, where you nearly broke down again when the waitress came back to tell you that the kitchen had run out of the dish you had ordered (displaced anguish in its most pronounced form—to such a degree that the nonsensical tears you felt gathering in your eyes might be interpreted as the very embodiment of repressed emotions that can no longer be repressed), and once the three of you had returned to the house, the gloom of a house shadowed in death, all of you convinced that these were the last days of your stepfather's life, you sat down at the dining room table to have a drink, and just when you thought it would be impossible for anyone to say another word, when the heaviness in your hearts seemed to have crushed all the words out of you, your mother started telling jokes. One joke and then another joke, then another joke followed by the next joke, jokes so funny that you and your wife laughed until you could hardly breathe anymore, an hour of jokes, two hours of jokes, each one delivered with such crackerjack timing, such crisp, economical language that a moment came when you thought your stomach might burst through your skin. Jewish jokes mostly, an unending torrent of classic yenta routines with all the appropriate voices and accents, the old Jewish women sitting around a card table and sighing, each one sighing in turn, each one sighing more loudly that the last, until one of the women finally says, "I thought we agreed not to talk about the children." You all went a little crazy that night, but the circumstances were so grim and intolerable that you needed to go a little crazy, and somehow your mother managed to find the strength to let that happen. A moment of extraordinary courage, you felt, a sublime instance of who she was at her best—for great as your misery was that night, you knew that it was nothing, absolutely nothing compared to hers.

He survived the Stanford Medical Center and went home, but less than a year later he was dead. You believe that was when she died as well. Her heart went on beating for another twenty years, but the death of your stepfather was the end of her, and she never regained her footing after that. Little by little, her grief was transformed into a kind of resentment (*How dare he die on me and leave me alone?*), and while it pained you to hear her talk like that, you understood that she was frightened, searching for a way to hazard the next step and hobble on toward the future. She hated living on her own, was temperamentally not equipped to survive in a vacuum of solitude, and before long she was back in circulation, quite heavy now, many pounds overweight, but still attractive enough to turn the heads of several aging men. She had been living in southern California for over a decade at that point, and you saw each other infrequently, no more than once every six months or so, and what you knew about her was learned mostly through telephone conversations—useful in their way, but you seldom had a chance to observe her in action, and consequently you were both surprised and not surprised when she told you she was planning to get married again after just eighteen months of widowhood. It was a foolish marriage in your opinion, another hasty, ill-considered marriage, not unlike the marriage she made with your father in 1946, but she wasn't looking for a big love anymore so much as a refuge, someone to take care of her as she mended her fragile self. In his quiet, fumbling way, the third husband was devoted to her, which certainly counts for something, but for all his efforts and good intentions, he couldn't take care of her well enough. He was a dull man, an ex-marine and former NASA engineer, conservative in both his politics and his manner, either meek or weak (perhaps both), and therefore a one-hundred-and-eighty-degree turn from your effusive, charismatic, left-liberal stepfather—not a bad or cruel person, simply dull. He now worked as a self-employed inventor (of the struggling variety), but your mother had high hopes for his most recent invention—an intravenous medical device, both tubeless and portable, that would compete with and potentially supplant the traditional IV—and because it looked like a sure thing, she married him on the assumption that they would soon be rolling in money. There is no doubt that it was a clever invention, perhaps even a brilliant one, but the inventor had no head for business. Squeezed between fast-talking venture capitalists and double-talking medical supply firms, he eventually lost control of his own device, and while he walked off with some money in the end, it was hardly enough to roll in—so little, in fact, that within a year most of it was gone. Your mother, who was into her sixties by then, was forced to go back to work. She restarted the interior design business she had shut down some years earlier, and with her inventor husband serving as her office assistant and bookkeeper, she was the one who was supporting them now, or trying to support them, and whenever their bank account was in danger of dipping toward zero, she would call you to ask for help, always tearful, always apologetic, and because you were in a position to give that help, you sent them checks every so often, some large checks, some small checks, about a dozen checks and wire transfers over the next couple of years. You didn't mind sending them the money, but you found it strange, and more than a little disheartening, that her ex-marine had given up on himself so thoroughly that he was no longer able to pull his weight, that the man who was going to provide for her and lead them into the bower of a comfortable old age could not even summon the courage to thank you for your help. Your mother was the boss now, and bit by bit his role as husband was turned into that of faithful butler (breakfast in bed, shopping for groceries), but still they forged on, it wasn't so bad, surely it could have been worse, and even if she was disappointed by the way things had turned out, she also knew that something was better than nothing. Then, one morning in the spring of 1994, just after she had woken up, your mother walked into the bathroom and found her husband lying dead on the floor. Stroke, heart attack, cerebral hemorrhage—it is impossible to say, since no autopsy was ever performed, at least none that you are aware of. When she called your house in Brooklyn later that morning, her voice was filled with horror. Blood, she said to you, blood coming out of his mouth, blood everywhere, and for the first time in all the years you had known her, she sounded deranged.

She decided to move back east. Twenty years earlier, she had thought of California as a promised land, but now it was little more than a place of disease and death, the capital of bad luck and painful memories, and so she bolted across America to be near her family—you and your wife to begin with, but also her mentally ill daughter in Connecticut, her sister, and her two grandchildren. She was flat broke, of course, which meant that you would have to support her, but that was hardly a problem now, and you were more than willing to do it. You bought her a one-bedroom apartment in Verona, leased a car for her, and gave her what you both considered to be an adequate monthly allowance. You were hardly the first son in the world to find himself in this position, but that didn't make it any less strange or uncomfortable: to be taking care of the person who had once taken care of you, to have reached that point in life when your roles were reversed, with you now acting the part of parent while she was reduced to the part of helpless child. The financial arrangement occasionally caused some friction, since your mother found it difficult not to overspend her allowance, and even though you increased the amount several times, it was still difficult for her, which put you in the awkward spot of having to scold her every now and then, and once, when you were probably a bit too harsh with her, she broke down and cried on the telephone, telling you she was a useless old woman and maybe she should kill herself so she wouldn't be such a burden anymore. There was something comical about this gush of self-pity (you knew you were being manipulated), but at the same time it made you feel wretched, and in the end you always caved in and let her have whatever she wanted. More worrisome to you was her inability to do anything, to get out of her apartment and engage herself with the world. You suggested that she volunteer as a reading teacher for struggling children or illiterate adults, get involved with the Democratic Party or some other political organization, take courses, travel, join a social club, but she simply didn't have it in her to try. Until then, the lack of a formal education had never been an impediment to her—her native intelligence and quickness had seemed to make up for any deficiencies—but now that she was without a husband, without work, without anything to keep her occupied from day to day, you wished she could have developed an interest in music or art or books, in anything really, just so long as it was some kind of passionate, sustaining interest, but she had never formed the habit of nurturing inner pursuits of that kind, and therefore she continued to flail around without purpose, never quite sure what to do with herself when she woke up in the morning. The only novels she read were detective stories and thrillers, and even your books and your wife's books, which you both automatically gave her whenever they were published—and which she proudly displayed on a special shelf in her living room—were not the sorts of books she could read. She watched a lot of television. The TV was always on in her apartment, blasting forth from early in the morning until late at night, but it wasn't for watching programs so much as for the voices that came from the box. Those voices comforted her, were in fact necessary to her, and they helped her overcome her fear of living alone—which was probably her single greatest accomplishment of those years. No, they were not the best years, but you don't want to give the impression that it was a time of unbroken melancholy and disarray. She made regular visits to Connecticut to see your sister, spent countless weekends with you at your house in Brooklyn, saw her granddaughter perform in school plays and sing her solos for the school chorus, followed her grandson's ever-deepening interest in photography, and after all those years in distant California, she was now a part of your life again, always present for birthdays, holidays, and special events—public appearances by you and your wife, the openings of your films (she was mad for the movies), and occasional dinners with your friends. She continued to charm people in public, even into her mid-seventies, for in some small corner of her mind she still saw herself as a star, as the most beautiful woman in the world, and whenever she emerged from her diminished, largely shut-in life, her vanity seemed to be intact. So much of what she had become saddened you now, but you found it impossible not to admire her for that vanity, for still being able to tell a good joke when people were listening.

You scattered her ashes in the woods of Prospect Park. There were five of you present that day—your wife, your daughter, your aunt, your cousin Regina, and yourself—and you chose Prospect Park in Brooklyn because your mother had played there often as a little girl. One by one, you all read poems out loud, and then, as you opened the rectangular metal urn and tossed the ashes onto the fallen leaves and underbrush, your aunt (normally undemonstrative, one of the most reserved people you have ever known) gave in to a fit of tears as she repeated the name of her baby sister over and over again. A week or two later, on a sparkling afternoon in late May, you and your wife took your dog for a walk in the park. You suggested returning to the spot where you had scattered your mother's ashes, but when you were still out on an open path, a good two hundred yards from the edge of the woods, you started feeling faint and dizzy, and even though you were taking pills to keep your new condition under control, you could feel another panic attack coming on. You took hold of your wife's arm, and the two of you turned around and went home. That was nearly nine years ago. You have not tried to go back to those woods since.

Summer 2010. Heat-wave weather, the Dog Star barking from sunup to sundown and on through the nights, a string of ninety-degree days and now, suddenly, all the way up to a hundred and six. It is a minute or two past midnight. Your wife has already gone to bed, but you are too restless for sleep, and so you have gone into the upstairs parlor, the room you both refer to as the library, an ample space with bookshelves lining three of the walls, and because those shelves are full now, crammed with the thousands of hardcovers and paperbacks you and your wife have accumulated over the years, there are piles of books and DVDs on the floor as well, the inevitable spillover that continues to grow as the months and years rush past you, giving the library a cluttered but sympathetic atmosphere of plenitude and well-being, the kind of room all visitors to the house describe as *cozy,* and yes, it is unquestionably your favorite room, with its soft leather couch and flat-screen TV, a perfect place for reading books and watching films, and because of the excruciating weather outside, the air-conditioning is on and the windows are closed, blocking out all sounds from the street, the nighttime medley of barking dogs and human voices, the weird, chubby man who wanders through the neighborhood singing show tunes in a piercing falsetto, the rumble of passing trucks, cars, and motorcycles. You turn on the television. The Mets game ended a couple of hours ago, and with no distraction available to you from the world of sport, you switch to the movie channel you like best, TCM, with its round-the-clock programming of old American films, and a few minutes into the story you have now begun to watch, something important occurs to you. It begins when you see the man running through the streets of San Francisco, a crazed man charging down the stone steps of the medical center and dashing out into the streets, a man with nowhere to go, running along crowded sidewalks, darting into traffic, bumping into people as he sprints past them, a cannonball of frenzy and disbelief who has just been told he will be dead within days, if not hours, that his body has been contaminated by a *luminous toxin*, and because it is too late to flush the poison from his system, there is no hope for him, and even if he still appears to be alive, he is in fact already dead, he has in fact been murdered.

You have been that man, you tell yourself, and what you are watching on the television screen is a precise rendering of what happened to you two days after your mother's death in 2002: the hammer that descends without warning, and then the inability to breathe, the pounding heart, the dizziness, the sweats, the body that falls to the floor, the arms and legs that turn to stone, the howls that blast forth from maddened, airless lungs, and the certainty that the end is upon you, that one second from now the world will no longer exist, because you will no longer exist.

Directed by Rudolph Maté in 1950, the film is called *D.O.A.*, police shorthand for *dead on arrival*, and the hero-victim is one Frank Bigelow, a man of no particular distinction or interest, a no one, an anyone, roughly thirty-five years old, an accountant, auditor, and notary public who lives in Banning, California, a small desert town near Palm Springs. Bulky of build, with a fleshy, full-lipped face, he is a man with little else on his mind but women, and because he is feeling suffocated by his adoring, neurotic, obsessively clinging secretary, Paula, the woman he might or might not be planning to marry, he impulsively decides to take a week off from work and go to San Francisco on a solo vacation. When he checks in at the St. Francis Hotel, the lobby is swarming with boisterous guests. It happens to be "market week," the desk clerk tells him, an annual convention of traveling salesmen, and each time an attractive woman saunters past (all the women in the hotel are attractive), Bigelow turns to ogle her with the wide-eyed, slack-jawed lust of a man on the prowl. To push home the point, each of these glances is accompanied by a comic, slide-whistle rendition of the standard two-note wolf call, as if to suggest that Bigelow can't quite believe his good luck, that by landing in this particular hotel on this particular day he will in all likelihood chance upon some easy action. When he goes up to his room on the sixth floor, the hallway is hopping with semi-inebriated revelers (more slide-whistle wolf calls) and the door of the room directly opposite is open, giving Bigelow a clear view of a full-scale bash in progress. So the vacation begins.

Paula has telephoned from Banning, and before Bigelow unpacks and settles in, he returns the call. It seems there has been an urgent message from someone named Eugene Philips of Los Angeles, who said it was imperative that Bigelow contact him *at once,* that they must talk *before it's too late.* Bigelow has no idea who Philips is. Have we done business with him? he asks Paula, but she has no memory of such a person either. All during this conversation, Bigelow is distracted by the goings-on across the hall. Women stop in his open doorway to wave hello and smile at him, and he waves and smiles back, even as he goes on talking to Paula. Forget about Philips, he tells her. He's on vacation now, he doesn't want to be bothered, and he'll deal with it when he returns to Banning.

After they hang up, Bigelow lights a cigarette, a waiter appears with a drink, and then a reveler from across the hall, who identifies himself as Haskell, enters the room and asks if he can use the phone. Three more bottles of bourbon and two more bottles of scotch are ordered for the party in 617. When Haskell learns that Bigelow is a stranger in town, he invites him to join in the merriment (*a few drinks, a few laughs*), and within two minutes Bigelow is dancing a rumba with Haskell's wife in the noisy room across the way. Sue is a brash, boozed-up piece of work, a frustrated woman looking for a good time, and because Bigelow turns out to be a skillful dancer, he becomes her number one target—not the most intelligent move, perhaps, given that her husband is right there to witness her antics, but Sue is both reckless and determined. Some minutes later, the gang from room 617 decides to leave the hotel and go out on the town. A reluctant Bigelow is dragged along with them, and suddenly they are in a crowded jazz club called the Fisherman, a frenetic place where an ensemble of black musicians is belting out an exultant, high-speed number with the word JIVE written on the wall behind them. One close-up after another shows the sax man, the piano man, the trumpet man, the bass man, and the drum man wailing on their instruments, intercut with wild reactions from the audience, and there is Bigelow sitting at the table with his new friends as the impetuous Sue clings tightly to him. Bigelow looks despondent, he is fed up, he wants no part of Sue or this cacophonous assault, and Haskell looks no less downhearted himself, studying his wife in silence as she throws herself at the stranger from across the hall. At some point in all this, the camera catches a man entering the club from behind, a tall man wearing a hat and an overcoat with an upturned collar, an odd and altogether curious collar, the reverse of which is marked by a black-and-white checkered pattern. The man approaches the bar, and a moment or two after that Bigelow finally manages to extricate himself from Sue and her companions. He goes to the bar as well and orders himself a bourbon, little knowing that the man with the curious collar is about to slip poison into his drink and that he, Bigelow, will be dead within twenty-four hours.

A stylish woman is sitting at the other end of the bar, and as Bigelow waits for his drink, he asks the bartender if the blonde is alone. The blonde turns out to be Jeanie, a *jive-crazy* rich girl who hangs out in clubs and uses words like *dig* and *easy* (i.e., copacetic, swell, no problem). Bigelow sidles over to her, and in those few seconds when he loses contact with his drink, which has now been poured and is waiting for him at his old spot at the other end of the bar, the man with the curious collar carries out his murderous mission, deftly pouring a measure of the toxic potion into the glass and then vanishing from sight. As Bigelow chats with the elegant Jeanie, who is at once cool and friendly, a self-possessed hipster queen, the bartender hands him his now doctored drink, his now deadly drink. Bigelow takes a sip, and instantly his face registers surprise, disgust. A second sip produces the same result. Pushing away the glass, he says to the bartender: "This isn't mine. I ordered bourbon. Give me another drink."

Meanwhile, Sue is on her feet, scanning the room for Bigelow, looking anxious, distraught, puzzled by his failure to return. Bigelow catches sight of her, then swings around and invites Jeanie to go somewhere else with him. There are people he wants to avoid, he says, and surely there must be other interesting places in San Francisco. Yes, Jeanie says, but she hasn't quite had her fill of the Fisherman. Why don't they meet up later when she hits her next spot of the evening, and then she writes down a telephone number on a piece of paper and tells him to call her there in an hour.

Bigelow returns to his hotel room, pulls out the scrap of paper with Jeanie's number on it, and picks up the phone, but before he can make the call, he glances up and sees that a bouquet of flowers has been delivered to the room. There is a card from Paula attached to the wrapping paper, and the message reads: *I'll keep a light burning in the window. Sweet dreams.* Bigelow is chastened. Instead of going out again to spend the night chasing skirts, he tears up Jeanie's number and tosses it in the trash, and a moment after that the story enters a different register, the real story begins.

The poison has already begun to do its work. Bigelow's head aches, but he assumes he has drunk too much and will feel better after he has slept it off. He climbs into bed, and as he does so the air fills with strange, disjointed sounds, the echoing voice of a distant female singer, mental debris from the jazz club, signs of mounting physical distress. When he wakes in the morning, Bigelow's condition has not improved. Still convinced that he drank too much and is suffering from a hangover, he calls room service and orders a pick-me-up, one of those tart, eye-opening nostrums spiced with horseradish and Worcestershire sauce that are supposed to jolt you into instant sobriety, but once the waiter shows up with the concoction, Bigelow can't face it, the mere sight of the drink fills him with nausea, and he asks the waiter to take it away. Something is seriously wrong. Bigelow clutches his stomach, appears dizzy and disoriented, and when the waiter asks if he is all right, the fatally ill victim-hero, still in the dark about what has befallen him, says he must have had too big a night of it and needs to get some fresh air.

Bigelow goes out, staggering ever so slightly, mopping his forehead with a handkerchief, and climbs onto a passing cable car. He jumps off at Nob Hill, and then he is walking, walking through deserted streets in broad daylight, walking with purpose, on his way somewhere—but what where and to what purpose?—until he finds the address he is looking for, a tall white structure with the words MEDICAL BUILDING chiseled into the stone façade. Bigelow is far more worried than he let on to the waiter at the hotel. He knows, indeed he knows, that something is seriously wrong with him.

At first, the results of the examination are encouraging. Looking at Bigelow's X-ray, a doctor says: "Lungs in good condition, blood pressure normal, heart fine. It's a good thing everybody isn't like you. It would put us doctors out of business." He instructs Bigelow to put on his clothes as they wait for the results of the blood tests administered by his colleague, Dr. Schaefer. As Bigelow knots his tie in the foreground, face to the camera, expressionless, a nurse walks into the room behind him, too addled to say a word, staring at him with a look that combines both horror and pity, and at that moment there can be no doubt that Bigelow is doomed. Dr. Schaefer enters, trying to mask his alarm. He and the first doctor confirm that Bigelow is unmarried, that he has no relatives in San Francisco, that he has come to the city alone. Why these questions? Bigelow asks. You're a very sick man, the doctor says. *You must steel yourself for a shock.* And then they tell him about the luminous toxic matter that has entered his system and will soon be attacking his vital organs. They wish there was something they could do, they say, but there is no antidote for this particular poison. He doesn't have long.

Bigelow is incredulous, filled with rage. This is impossible! he shouts. They must be wrong, there must be an error, but the doctors calmly defend their diagnosis, assuring him that there hasn't been an error—which only increases Bigelow's fury. "You're telling me I'm dead!" he roars. "I don't even know who you are! Why should I believe you?" Calling them both crazy, he pushes them aside and storms out of the office.

Cut to an even larger building—a hospital? another

medical center?—and a shot of Bigelow bounding up the front steps. He barges into a room marked EMERGENCY, apoplectic, a man about to explode into a hundred fragments, and shoves his way past two bewildered and frightened nurses, insisting that he see a doctor at once, demanding that someone examine him for luminous poison.

The new doctor comes to the same conclusion as the first pair. *You've got it, all right. Your system has already absorbed it.* To prove the point, he switches off the overhead light and shows Bigelow the test tube containing the examination results. It is an eerie sight. The thing glows in the dark—as if the doctor were holding a vial of incandescent milk, a frosted bulb filled with radium, or worse, the liquefied fallout from a nuclear bomb. Bigelow's anger subsides. Faced with such overpowering evidence, he temporarily goes numb. "But I don't feel sick," he says quietly. "Just a little stomachache, that's all."

The doctor warns him not to be fooled by his apparent lack of symptoms. Bigelow has no more than a day or two to live, a week at the most. *There's nothing that can be done now.* Then the doctor learns that Bigelow has no idea how, when, or where he swallowed the poison, which means that it was administered by another party, an unknown party, which further means that someone intentionally set out to kill him.

"This is a case for Homicide," the doctor says, reaching for the telephone.

"Homicide?"

"I don't think you understand, Bigelow. You've been murdered."

This is the moment when Bigelow snaps, when the monstrous thing that has happened to him turns into an all-out, unbridled panic, when the howl of agony begins. He bursts out of the doctor's office, bursts out of the building, and starts running through the streets, and as you follow this passage of the film, this long sequence of shots tracking Bigelow's mad fugue through the city, you understand that you are witnessing the outer manifestation of an inner state, that this senseless, headlong, unstoppable running is nothing less than the depiction of a mind filled with horror, that you are watching the choreography of dread. A panic attack has been translated into a breathless sprint through the streets of a city, for panic is nothing if not an expression of mental flight, the unbidden force that grows inside you when you are trapped, when the truth is too much to bear, when the injustice of this unavoidable truth can no longer be confronted, and therefore the only possible response is to flee, to shut down your mind by transforming yourself into a gasping, twitching, delirious body, and what truth could be more terrible than this one? Condemned to death within hours or days, cut down in the middle of your life for reasons that entirely escape your understanding, your life suddenly reduced to a thimbleful of minutes, seconds, heartbeats.

It doesn't matter what happens next. You watch the second half of the film attentively, but you know the story is over, that even as the story continues, there is nothing left to say. Bigelow will spend his last hours on earth trying to solve the mystery of his murder. He will learn that Philips, the man who called his office from Los Angeles, is dead. He will go to Los Angeles and investigate the activities of various thieves, psychopaths, and two-faced women. He will be shot at and punched. He will learn that his involvement in the story is purely accidental, that the villains want him dead because he happened to notarize a bill of sale pertaining to a stolen shipment of iridium and he is the only man alive who can identify the culprits. He will track down his murderer, the man with the curious collar, who is also the murderer of Philips, and kill him in a shoot-out on the landing of a darkened stairway. And then, shortly after that, Bigelow himself will die, just as the doctors said he would—in mid-sentence, telling his story to the police.

There is nothing wrong with playing it out like this, you suppose. It is the conventional thing to do, the manly, heroic option, the trope that befits all adventure stories, but why, you wonder, does Bigelow never divulge his imminent fate to anyone, not even to his doting, lovesick Paula? Perhaps because heroes must remain tough until the bitter end, and even when time is running out, they can't allow themselves to get bogged down in useless sentiment.

But you aren't tough anymore, are you? Ever since the panic attack of 2002, you have stopped being tough, and even though you work hard at trying to be a decent person, it has been a long time now since you last thought of yourself as heroic. If you ever found yourself in Bigelow's shoes, you are certain you would never do what Bigelow did. You would run through the streets, yes, you would run until you could no longer take another step, no longer breathe, no longer stand up, and then what? Call Paula, call Paula the instant you stopped running, but if her number happened to be busy when you called, then what? Prostrate yourself on the ground and weep, cursing the world for allowing you to have been born. Or else, quite simply, crawl off into a hole somewhere and wait to die.

You can't see yourself. You know what you look like because of mirrors and photographs, but out there in the world, as you move among your fellow human beings, whether friends or strangers or the most intimate beloveds, your own face is invisible to you. You can see other parts of yourself, arms and legs, hands and feet, shoulders and torso, but only from the front, nothing of the back except the backs of your legs if you twist them into the right position, but not your face, never your face, and in the end—at least as far as others are concerned—your face is who you are, the essential fact of your identity. Passports do not contain pictures of hands and feet. Even you, who have lived inside your body for sixty-four years now, would probably be unable to recognize your foot in an isolated photograph of that foot, not to speak of your ear, or your elbow, or one of your eyes in close-up. All so familiar to you in the context of the whole, but utterly anonymous when taken piece by piece. We are all aliens to ourselves, and if we have any sense of who we are, it is only because we live inside the eyes of others. Think of what happened to you when you were fourteen. For two weeks at the end of the summer, you worked for your father in Jersey City, joining one of the small crews that repaired and maintained the apartment buildings he and his brothers owned and managed: painting walls and ceilings, mending roofs, hammering nails into two-by-fours, pulling up sheets of cracked linoleum. The two men you worked with were black, every tenant in every apartment was black, every person in the neighborhood was black, and after two weeks of looking at nothing but black faces, you began to forget that your own face wasn't black. Since you couldn't see your own face, you saw yourself in the faces of the people around you, and bit by bit you stopped thinking of yourself as different. In effect, you stopped thinking about yourself at all.

Looking at your right hand as it grips the black fountain pen you are using to write this journal, you think of Keats looking at his own right hand under similar circumstances, in the act of writing one of his last poems and suddenly breaking off to scribble eight lines in the margin of the manuscript, the bitter outcry of a young man who knew he was headed for an early grave, darkly underscored by the word *now* in the first line, for every *now* necessarily implies a *later*, and what *later* could Keats look forward to but the prospect of his own death?

This living hand, now warm and capable
Of earnest grasping, would, if it were cold
And in the icy silence of the tomb,
So haunt thy days and chill thy dreaming nights
That thou would wish thine own heart dry of blood
So in my veins red life might stream again,
And thou be conscience-calm'd—see here it is—
I hold it toward you.

Keats to begin with, but no sooner do you think of *This living hand* than you are reminded of a story someone once told you about James Joyce, Joyce in Paris in the 1920s, standing around at a party eighty-five years ago when a woman walked up to him and asked if she could shake the hand that wrote *Ulysses*. Instead of offering her his right hand, Joyce lifted it in the air, studied it for a few moments, and said: "Let me remind you, madam, that this hand has done many other things as well." No details given, but what a delicious piece of smut and innuendo, all the more effective because he left everything to the woman's imagination. What did he want her to see? Wiping his ass, probably, picking his nose, masturbating in bed at night, sticking his fingers into Nora's cunt and diddling her bunghole, popping pimples, scraping food from his teeth, plucking out nostril hairs, disgorging wax from his ears—fill in the appropriate blanks, the central point being: whatever was most disgusting to her. Your hands have served you in similar ways, of course, everyone's hands have done those things, but mostly they are busy performing tasks that require little or no thought. Opening and closing doors, screwing light bulbs into sockets, dialing telephones, washing dishes, turning the pages of books, holding your pen, brushing your teeth, drying your hair, folding towels, taking money out of your wallet, carrying bags of groceries, swiping your MetroCard in subway turnstiles, pushing buttons on machines, picking up the newspaper from the front steps in the morning, turning down the covers of the bed, showing your ticket to the train conductor, flushing the toilet, lighting your little cigars, stubbing out your little cigars in ashtrays, putting on your pants, taking off your pants, tying your shoes, squirting shaving cream onto the tips of your fingers, clapping at plays and concerts, sliding keys into locks, scratching your face, scratching your arm, scratching your ass, wheeling suitcases through airports, unpacking suitcases, putting your shirts on hangers, zipping up your fly, buckling your belt, buttoning your jacket, knotting your tie, drumming your fingers on tables, loading paper into your fax machine, tearing checks out of your checkbook, opening up boxes of tea, switching on lights, switching off lights, plumping up your pillow before going to bed. Those same hands have sometimes punched people (as previously noted), and three or four times, in moments of intense frustration, they have also punched walls. They have thrown plates onto the floor, dropped plates onto the floor, and picked up plates from the floor. Your right hand has shaken more hands than you could possibly count, has blown your nose, wiped your ass, and waved good-bye more often than the number of words in the largest dictionary. Your hands have held the bodies of your children, have wiped the asses and blown the noses of your children, have bathed your children, rubbed the backs of your children, dried the tears of your children, and stroked the faces of your children. They have patted the shoulders of friends, work comrades, and relatives. They have pushed and shoved, pulled people off the ground, gripped the arms of people who were about to fall, navigated the wheelchairs of those who could not walk. They have touched the bodies of clothed and naked women. They have moved down the length of your wife's naked skin and found their way onto every part of her. They are happiest there, you feel, have always been happiest there since the day you met her, for, to paraphrase a line from one of George Oppen's poems, some of the most beautiful places in the world are on your wife's body.

The day after the car crash in 2002, you went to the junkyard where the car had been towed to retrieve your daughter's belongings. It was a Sunday morning in August, warm as always, with a misty blur of rain dappling the streets as one of your friends drove you out to some godforsaken neighborhood in Brooklyn, a no-man's-land of crumbling warehouses, vacant lots, and boarded-up wooden buildings. The junkyard was run by a black man in his mid-sixties, a smallish fellow with long dreadlocks and clear, steady eyes, a gentle Rasta man who watched over his domain of wrecked automobiles like a shepherd tending a flock of dozing sheep. You told him why you were there, and when he led you over to the shiny new Toyota you had been driving the day before, you were stunned by how thoroughly destroyed it was, could not fathom how you and your family had managed to survive such a catastrophe. Immediately after the crash, you had noticed how badly damaged the car was, but you had been rattled by the collision, were not fully able to absorb what had happened to you, but now, a day later, you could see that the metal body of the car was so smashed in, it looked like a piece of crumpled paper. "Look at that," you said to the Rasta man. "We should all be dead now." He studied the car for a few seconds, looked you in the eye, and then turned his head upward as the fine rain fell onto his face and abundant hair. "An angel was watching over you," he said in a quiet voice. "You were supposed to die yesterday, but then an angel stretched out his hand and pulled you back into the world." He delivered those words with such serenity and conviction, you almost believed him.

When you sleep, you sleep soundly, seldom stirring until it is time to wake up in the morning. The problem you occasionally run into, however, is a reluctance to go to bed in the first place, a late-night surge of energy that prevents you from wanting to call it quits until you have polished off another chapter of the book you are reading, or watched a film on television, or, if it is baseball season and the Mets or the Yankees are playing on the West Coast, tuned in the broadcast from San Francisco, Oakland, or Los Angeles. Afterward, you crawl into bed beside your wife, and within ten minutes you are dead to the world until morning. Nevertheless, every now and then, something will interfere with your normally profound slumbers. If you accidentally wind up on your back, for example, you might begin to snore, in all likelihood you will begin to snore, and if the noise you produce is loud enough to wake your wife, she will softly urge you to roll over, and if that benign tactic should fail, she will give you a shove, or shake your shoulder, or pinch your ear. Nine times out of ten, you will unconsciously do what she commands, and she will quickly fall back to sleep. The other ten percent of the time, her shove will wake you up, and because you don't want to trouble her sleep any further, you will go down the hall to the library and stretch out on the sofa, which is long enough to accommodate your fully extended body. More often than not, you manage to fall back asleep on the sofa—but sometimes you don't. Over the years, your sleep has also been broken by flies and mosquitoes buzzing in the room (the perils of summer), inadvertent punches in the face from your wife, who tends to fling out her arms when she rolls over in bed, and once, just once, you were rousted from your dreams when your wife started singing in the middle of one of her own dreams—belting out the lyrics of a song from a movie she had seen as a child, your brilliant, erudite, supremely sophisticated wife returning to her midwestern childhood with a splendid, full-voiced rendition of "Supercalifragilisticexpialidocious" as sung by Julie Andrews in *Mary Poppins*. One of the rare instances when the eight-year difference in your ages has ever been apparent to you, since you were too old for that film when it came out and therefore (mercifully) have never seen it.

But what to do when it is the middle of the night, when you have woken up sometime between two and four in the morning, have stretched out on the sofa in the library, and are unable to go back to sleep? It is too late to read, too late to turn on the television, too late to watch a film, and so you lie in the dark and ruminate, letting your thoughts go wherever they choose to go. Sometimes you get lucky and are able to latch onto a word, or a character, or a scene from the book you are working on, but more often you will discover yourself thinking about the past, and in your experience, whenever your thoughts turn to the past at three o'clock in the morning, those thoughts tend to be dark. One memory haunts you above all others, and on nights when you are unable to sleep, you find it difficult not to go back to it, to rehash the events of that day and relive the shame you felt afterward, have continued to feel ever since. It was thirty-two years ago, the morning of your father's funeral, and at some point you found yourself standing next to one of your uncles (the father of the cousin who called you on the morning of your panic attack), the two of you shaking hands with a line of mourners who shuffled past you as they offered their condolences, the ritual handshakes and empty words that punctuate every funeral service. Family members mostly, friends of your father's, men and women, faces you recognized and didn't recognize, and then you were shaking hands with Tom, one of the faces you didn't recognize, who told you he had been your father's chief electrician for many years and that your father had always treated him well, he was a good man, he said, this small Irishman with his Jersey City accent was telling you that your father was a good man, and you thanked him for that, you shook his hand again for that, and then he moved on to shake your uncle's hand, and when your uncle saw him, he immediately told Tom to leave, this was a private family funeral, he said, no outsiders were allowed, and when Tom mumbled that he only wanted to pay his respects, your uncle said sorry, he would have to leave, and so Tom turned around and left. Their conversation lasted no more than fifteen or twenty seconds, and you barely registered what was happening before Tom was on his way out. When you finally realized what your uncle had done, you were filled with disgust, appalled that he could have treated a person like that, any person, but especially this person, who was there only because he felt it was his duty to be there, and what still galls you today, what still floods you with shame, is that you said nothing to your uncle. Never mind that he was a man with a notorious temper, a hothead given to explosive rages and monumental shouting fits, and that if you had confronted him then, there was every chance he would have turned on you in the middle of your father's funeral. But so what? You should have confronted him, you should have had the courage to shout back at him if he had started shouting at you, and if not that, then why at least didn't you run after Tom and tell him he could stay? You have no idea why you didn't take a stand at that moment, and the shock of your father's sudden death is no excuse. You should have acted, and you didn't. All your life, you had been sticking up for people who had been pushed around, it was the one principle you believed in above all others, but on that particular day you held your tongue and did nothing. When you look back on it now, you understand that this failure to act is the reason why you have stopped thinking of yourself as heroic: because there was no excuse.

Nine years earlier (1970), while serving on the crew of the S.S. *Esso Florence,* you threatened to punch and even kill one of your shipmates for baiting you with anti-Semitic insults. You grabbed hold of his shirt, slammed him into a wall, and brought your right fist up against his face, telling him to stop calling you names or else. Martinez backed down immediately, apologized, and before long you became good friends. (Shades of Madame Rubinstein.) Nine years later, meaning nine years after your father's funeral (1988), you almost punched someone again, which was the last time you came close to engaging in a fight similar to the ones you fought as a boy. It was in Paris, and you remember the date well: September first, a special day on the French calendar, *la rentrée,* the official end of the summer holiday season, and therefore a day of crowds and inordinate confusion. For six weeks prior to that, you and your wife and children had been staying at your French publisher's house in the south, about fifteen kilometers east of Arles. It had been a restful time for all of you, a month and a half of quiet and work, of long walks and rambling excursions through the white hills of the Alpilles, of outdoor dinners under the plane tree in the yard, probably the most enjoyable summer of your life, with the added pleasure of seeing your one-year-old daughter take her first tottering steps without holding on to her parents' hands. You must not have been thinking clearly when you scheduled your return to Paris on September first, or perhaps you simply didn't understand what would be waiting for you when you got there. You had already put your eleven-year-old son on a plane back to New York (a direct flight from Nice), and so there were just three of you traveling north on the train that day, you and your wife and small daughter, along with a summer's worth of baggage and half a ton of baby supplies. You were looking forward to arriving in Paris, however, since your publisher had told you that an extensive article about your work would be appearing in that afternoon's *Le Monde*, and you wanted to buy a copy of the paper as soon as you climbed off the train. (You no longer read articles about yourself, no longer read reviews of your books, but this was then, and you still hadn't learned that ignoring what people say about you is beneficial to a writer's mental health.) The trip by T.G.V. from Avignon was a bit frazzling, largely because your daughter was too impressed by the high-speed train to sit still or sleep, which meant that you spent most of the three hours walking up and down the aisles of the cars with her, and by the time you pulled into the Gare de Lyon, you were ready for a nap. The station was mobbed with people, large masses of travelers surging forth in all directions, and you had to jostle and fight your way to the exit, your wife carrying the baby in her arms and you doing your best to push and pull the family's three large suitcases—not the easiest task, given that you had only two hands. In addition, there was a canvas bag slung over your shoulder, which held the first seventy-five pages of your novel in progress, and when you stopped to buy a copy of *Le Monde*, you slipped it into the bag as well. You wanted to read the article, of course, but after checking to see that it had indeed been printed in that afternoon's edition, you put it away, assuming you could take a closer look at it while you were waiting in line for a taxi. Once the three of you made it through the exit door, however, you discovered that there was no line. There were taxis in front of the station, there were people waiting for those taxis, but there was no line. The crowd was immense, and unlike the English, who are in the habit of queuing up whenever more than three of them are present and who then stand there patiently until it is their turn, or even the Americans, who go about it more sloppily but always with an innate sense of justice and fair play, the French turn into fractious children whenever there are too many of them gathered in a confined space, and rather than collectively try to impose some order on the situation, it suddenly becomes every man for himself. The pandemonium in front of the Gare de Lyon that day reminded you of certain news clips you have seen of the New York Stock Exchange: Black Tuesday, Black Friday, the international markets are crashing, the world is in ruins, and there, on the floor of the exchange, a thousand frantic men are screaming their lungs out, each one about to drop dead of a heart attack. Such was the crowd you had joined that September first twenty-two and a half years ago: the rabble were on the loose and no one was in charge, and there you were, no more than a stone's throw from where the Bastille had once stood, stormed two centuries earlier by a mob no less unruly than this one, but revolution wasn't in the air just now, what the people wanted wasn't bread or freedom but *taxis,* and since the taxi supply was less than a fiftieth of what it should have been, the people were fuming, the people were shouting, the people were ready to tear one another apart. Your wife was calm, you remember, amused by the spectacle unfolding around her, and even your little daughter was calm, taking in everything with her big, curious eyes, but you were becoming aggravated, you have always been at your worst when traveling, edgy and irritable and never quite yourself, and more than anything you hate being trapped in the chaos of crowds, and therefore, as you sized up the predicament you had fallen into, you concluded that the three of you would have to wait there for a good hour or two before finding a cab, perhaps six hours, perhaps a hundred hours, and so you said to your wife that maybe it wouldn't be a bad idea to look for a taxi somewhere else. You pointed to another taxi stand down the hill, a few hundred yards away. "But what about the bags?" she said. "You'll never be able to carry three heavy bags all the way over there." "Don't worry," you said. "I can handle it." Of course you couldn't handle it, or could just barely handle it, and after lugging those monsters for just twenty or thirty yards, you understood that you had vastly overestimated your own strength, but at that point it would have been foolish to turn back, and so you kept on going, pausing every ten seconds to reorganize the load, switching the two bags and the one bag from your left arm to your right arm, from your right arm to your left arm, sometimes putting one of them on your back and carrying the other two with your hands, continually shifting the weight, which must have totaled about a hundred pounds, and naturally enough you were starting to sweat, your pores were gushing in the heat of the afternoon sun, and by the time you made it to the next taxi stand, you were thoroughly exhausted. "You see," you said to your wife, "I told you I could do it." She smiled at you in the way one smiles at an imbecilic ten-year-old, for the truth was, even though you had made it to the next taxi stand, there were no taxis waiting there, since every driver in the city was headed for the Gare de Lyon. Nothing to be done now except hang around and hope that one of them would eventually come your way. The minutes passed, your body started cooling down to more or less its normal temperature, and then, just as an approaching taxi came into view, you and your wife saw a woman walking in your direction, a young, extremely tall African woman dressed in colorful African clothes and walking with perfectly erect posture, a small baby sleeping in a sling that was wrapped around her chest, a heavy bag of groceries hanging from her right hand, another heavy bag hanging from her left hand, and a third bag of groceries balanced on the top of her head. You were looking at a vision of human grace, you realized, the slow, fluid motion of her swaying hips, the slow, fluid motion of her walk, a woman bearing her burdens with what appeared to you as a kind of wisdom, the weight of each thing evenly distributed, her neck and head utterly still, her arms utterly still, the baby asleep on her chest, and after your embarrassing display of ineptitude as you hauled your own family's bags to this spot, you felt ridiculous in her presence, awed that a fellow human being could have mastered so well the very thing you yourself could not do. She was still walking toward you when the taxi pulled up and came to a stop. Relieved and happy now, you loaded the suitcases into the trunk and then slid into the backseat beside your wife and daughter. "Where to?" the driver asked, and when you told him where you were going, he shook his head and told you to get out of the cab. At first you didn't understand. "What are you talking about?" you said. "I'm talking about the trip," he replied. "It's too short, and I'm not going to waste my time on a measly fare like that." "Don't worry," you said. "I'll give you a good tip." "I don't care about your tip," he said. "I just want you out of the cab—now." "Are you blind?" you said. "We have a baby and a hundred pounds of luggage. What do you expect us to do—walk?" "That's your problem, not mine," he answered. "Out." There was nothing left to say to him. If the bastard in the front seat wouldn't take you to the address you had given him, what choice did you have but to get out of the taxi, unload your bags from the trunk, and wait for another cab? You were seething with anger by then, as angry and frustrated as you had been in years, no, more angry, more frustrated, more outraged than at any time you could remember, and when you had removed the bags from the trunk and the taxi man had started to drive away, you took the canvas bag that was slung over your shoulder, the bag that contained the only copy of the manuscript you were working on, not to mention the article in *Le Monde* that you were so anxious to read, and hurled it in the direction of the departing taxi. It landed with a great thud on the trunk of the car—a deeply satisfying thud that carried all the force of an exclamation mark set in fifty-point type. The driver slammed on the brakes, got out of the taxi, and began walking toward you with clenched fists, shouting at you for having attacked his precious vehicle, itching for a fight. You clenched your own fists and shouted back, warning him not to take another step toward you, or else you would dismantle him piece by piece and kick his sorry ass into the gutter. When you spoke those words, you had no doubt that you were prepared to tangle with him, that nothing was going to stop you from carrying out your promise to destroy this man, and when he looked into your eyes and saw that you meant what you were saying, he turned around, climbed into his cab, and drove off. You went out into the street to fetch your bag, and just then, as you bent down to pick it up, you saw the young African woman walking down the sidewalk with her baby and her three heavy bundles, well past you now, perhaps ten or twenty feet beyond where you were standing, and as you watched her move into the distance, you studied her slow and even gait, marveling at the stillness of her body, understanding that beyond the gentle swaying of her hips, not one part of her was moving except her legs.

One broken bone. Considering the thousands of games you took part in as a boy, you are surprised that there weren't others, at least several others. Twisted ankles, bruised thighs, sprained wrists, tender knees, sore elbows, shin splints, clunks on the head, but only one broken bone, your left shoulder, incurred during a football game when you were fourteen, which has prevented you from fully raising your arm for the past fifty years, but nothing of any great consequence, and you probably wouldn't bother to mention it now if not for the role your mother played in the story, which makes it her story in the end and not the story of how you, as the quarterback of your ninth-grade team, went diving for a fumbled ball in the backfield and wound up breaking your shoulder all by yourself, with no help from any of the players on the other team, leaping too far in your eagerness to recover the ball and landing in the wrong spot, on the wrong spot, and thereby breaking your bone when you crashed onto the hard ground. It was a frigid afternoon in late November, a game without referees or adult supervision, and after you hurt yourself you stood on the sideline and watched the rest of the game, disappointed that you couldn't play anymore, not yet understanding that your bone was broken but realizing that the injury was a bad one because you could no longer move your arm without feeling acute pain. Afterward, you hitchhiked back to your house with one of your friends, both of you still in your football uniforms, and you remember how difficult it was for you to remove your jersey and shoulder pads, so difficult in fact that you couldn't do it without your friend's help. It was a Saturday, and the house was empty. Your sister was off somewhere with friends, your father was at work, and your mother was at work as well, since Saturday was always a busy day for showing houses to prospective buyers. About two minutes after your friend helped you take off your shoulder pads, the telephone rang, and your friend went to answer it because you were finding it hard to move now without increasing the pain. It was your mother, and the first thing she said to your friend was: "Is Paul all right?" "Well," he answered, "not so good, actually. He seems to have hurt his arm." And then your mother said: "I knew it. That's why I called—because I've been worried." She told your friend that she was coming straight home and hung up. Later on, when she was driving you to the doctor for X-rays, she told you that a feeling had come over her that afternoon, a strange feeling that something had happened to you, and when you asked her when she had felt this feeling, it turned out that she had started worrying about you at the precise moment when you were diving onto the ground and breaking your shoulder.

You have no use for the *good old days*. Whenever you find yourself slipping into a nostalgic frame of mind, mourning the loss of the things that seemed to make life better then than it is now, you tell yourself to stop and think carefully, to look back at Then with the same scrutiny you apply to looking at Now, and before long you come to the conclusion that there is little difference between them, that the Now and the Then are essentially the same. Of course you have manifold grievances against the evils and stupidities of contemporary American life, not a day goes by when you are not wailing forth your harangues against the ascendency of the right, the injustices of the economy, the neglect of the environment, the collapsing infrastructure, the senseless wars, the barbarism of legalized torture and extraordinary rendition, the disintegration of impoverished cities like Buffalo and Detroit, the erosion of the labor movement, the debt we saddle our children with in order to attend our too-expensive colleges, the ever-growing crevasse that divides the rich from the poor, not to speak of the junk films we are making, the junk food we are eating, the junk thoughts we are thinking. It is enough to make one want to start a revolution—or live as a hermit in the Maine woods, feeding off berries and the roots of trees. And yet, go back to the year of your birth and try to remember what America looked like in its golden age of postwar prosperity: Jim Crow laws in full force throughout the South, anti-Semitic quota restrictions, back-alley abortions, Truman's executive order to establish a loyalty oath for all government workers, the trials of the Hollywood Ten, the Cold War, the Red Scare, the Bomb. Every moment in history is fraught with its own problems, its own injustices, and every period manufactures its own legends and pieties. You were sixteen when Kennedy was assassinated, a junior in high school, and the legend now says that the entire American population was bludgeoned into a state of wordless grief by the trauma that occurred on November twenty-second. You have another story to tell, however, for you and two of your friends happened to travel down to Washington on the day of the funeral. You wanted to be there because of your admiration for Kennedy, who had represented such a startling change after eight long years of Eisenhower, but you also wanted to be there because you were curious to know what it would feel like to participate in a *historical event*. It was the Sunday after the Friday, the day Ruby shot and killed Oswald, and you imagined that the crowds of onlookers lining the avenues as the funeral procession passed by would stand there in respectful silence, *in a state of wordless grief*, but what you encountered that afternoon was a throng of rowdy, rubbernecking gawkers, people perched in trees with their cameras, people shoving others out of the way to get a better look, and more than anything else, what you were reminded of was the atmosphere at a public hanging, the thrill that attends the spectacle of violent death. You were there, you witnessed those things with your own eyes, and yet in all the years since then, not once have you heard anyone talk about what really happened.

Nevertheless, there are things you miss from the old days, even if you have no desire to see those days return. The ring of the old telephones, the clacking of typewriters, milk in bottles, baseball without designated hitters, vinyl records, galoshes, stockings and garter belts, black-and-white movies, heavyweight champions, the Brooklyn Dodgers and the New York Giants, paperback books for thirty-five cents, the political left, Jewish dairy restaurants, double features, basketball before the three-point shot, palatial movie houses, nondigital cameras, toasters that lasted for thirty years, contempt for authority, Nash Ramblers, and wood-paneled station wagons. But there is nothing you miss more than the world as it was before smoking was banned in public places. From your first cigarette at age sixteen (in Washington with your friends at Kennedy's funeral) until the end of the previous millennium, you were free—with just a few exceptions—to smoke anywhere you liked. Restaurants and bars to begin with, but also college classrooms, movie theater balconies, bookstores and record stores, doctors' waiting rooms, taxicabs, ballparks and indoor arenas, elevators, hotel rooms, trains, long-distance buses, airports, airplanes, and the shuttle buses at airports that took you to the planes. The world is probably better off now with its militant anti-smoking laws, but something has also been lost, and whatever that thing is (a sense of ease? tolerance of human frailty? conviviality? an absence of puritanical anguish?), you miss it.

Some memories are so strange to you, so unlikely, so outside the realm of the plausible, that you find it difficult to reconcile them with the fact that you are the person who experienced the events you are remembering. At the age of seventeen, for example, on a flight from Milan to New York after your first trip abroad (to visit your mother's sister in Italy, where she had been living for the past eleven years), you sat next to an attractive, highly intelligent girl of eighteen or nineteen, and after an hour of conversation, you spent the rest of the journey kissing each other with lustful abandon, necking passionately in front of the other passengers without the slightest hint of shame or self-consciousness. It seems impossible that this could have happened, but it did. Even stranger, on the last morning of your European jaunt the following year, the one that began by crossing the Atlantic on the student ship, you boarded a plane at Shannon Airport in Ireland and found yourself sitting next to another pretty girl. After an hour of serious conversation about books, colleges, and your summer adventures, the two of you began necking as well, going at each other so fiercely that eventually you covered yourselves with a blanket, and under that blanket you moved your hands all over her body and up into her skirt, and it was only by sheer force of will that the two of you restrained yourselves from venturing into the forbidden territory of out-and-out fucking. How was it possible that such a thing could have happened? Are the sexual energies of youth so powerful that the mere presence of another body can serve as an inducement to sex? You would never do such a thing now, would not even dare to think of doing such a thing—but then again, you are no longer young.

No, you were never promiscuous, even if you sometimes wish you had allowed yourself to be wilder and more impulsive, but in spite of your temperate behavior, you had a couple of run-ins with the dreaded germs of intimacy. The clap. It happened to you once, when you were twenty years old, and once was more than enough. A viscous green slime oozing from the tip of your cock, a feeling that a metal pin had been jammed down your urethra, and the simple act of urination turned into an agony. You never knew how you contracted gonorrhea, the cast of possible candidates was limited, and none of them struck you as a likely carrier of that dismal scourge, but five years later, when you found yourself with a case of the crabs, you did know who was responsible. No pain this time, but an incessant itch in the pubic region, and when you finally looked down to see what was going on, you were astonished to discover that you had been infested with a battalion of midget crabs—identical in shape to the crabs that live in the ocean, but minute in size, no bigger than ladybugs. You were so ignorant about venereal diseases that you had never heard of this affliction until you caught it yourself, had no idea that such a thing as the crab louse even existed. Penicillin had cured the gonorrhea, but nothing more than a powder was needed to rid you of the vermin who were camping out in your pubes. A minor complaint, then, rather comical when looked at from a distance, but at the time you found it sad, deeply sad, for the person who had contaminated you with those itchy devils had been the first great love of your life, the mad love that had struck you down at fifteen and had tortured you through the remaining years of your adolescence, and sleeping with her now, in your early adulthood, had made you feel that perhaps you were destined to love her again and that this time—if the gods were with you—your love would be fully requited. But the clandestine weekend you had spent together was not the beginning of a new story. It was the end of an old story—a happy end in its own way, but still the end, the very end, and the bugs crawling around in your crotch were nothing more than a sad little coda to that final chapter.

Ladybugs were considered good luck. If one of them landed on your arm, you were supposed to make a wish before it flew away. Four-leaf clovers were also agents of good fortune, and you spent countless hours in your early childhood on your hands and knees in the grass, searching for those small prizes, which did indeed exist but were found only rarely and therefore were a cause for much celebration. Spring was heralded by the appearance of the first robin, the brown, red-breasted bird who would suddenly and unaccountably show up in your backyard one morning, hopping around on the grass and digging for worms. You would count the robins after that, taking note of the second one, the third one, the fourth one, adding more robins to the tally each day, and by the time you stopped counting them, the weather would be warm. The first summer after you moved into the house on Irving Avenue (1952), your mother planted a garden in the backyard, and among the clusters of annuals and perennials in the loamy earth of the flower bed, there was a single sunflower, which continued to grow as the weeks went by, first coming up to your shins, then up to your waist, then up to your shoulders, and then, after reaching the top of your head, shooting on past you to a height of about six feet. The sunflower's progress was the central event of the summer, a bracing plunge into the mysterious workings of time, and every morning you would run into the backyard to measure yourself against it and see how fast it was gaining on you. That same summer, you made your first close friend, the first true comrade of your childhood, a boy named Billy whose house was just a short distance from yours, and because you were the only person who could understand him when he talked (he garbled his words, which seemed to sink back into his saliva-clogged mouth before they could emerge as cleanly articulated sound), he relied on you as his interpreter to the rest of the world, and you relied on him as an intrepid Huck to your more cautious Tom. The next spring, you spent every afternoon combing through the bushes together, looking for dead birds—mostly fledglings, you now realize, who must have fallen out of their nests and could not make their way back home. You buried them in a patch of dirt that ran along the side of your house—intensely solemn rituals accompanied by made-up prayers and long moments of silence. You had both discovered death by then, and you knew that it was a serious business, something that did not allow for any jokes.

The first human death your remember with any clarity took place in 1957, when your eighty-year-old grandmother dropped down on the floor with a heart attack and died in a hospital later that day. You have no memory of going to the funeral, which would suggest you were not there, in all likelihood because you were ten years old and your parents thought you were too young. What you remember is the darkness that filled the house for days afterward, the people coming and going to sit shiva with your father in the living room, unknown men reciting incomprehensible Hebrew prayers in mumbled voices, the strangely quiet commotion of it all, your father's grief. You yourself were almost entirely untouched by this death. You had felt no connection to your grandmother, no love from her, no curiosity about who you were, not the slightest glimmer of affection, and the few times she'd wrapped her arms around you for a grandmotherly hug, you had felt frightened, eager for the embrace to end. The 1919 murder was still a family secret then, you would not learn about it until you were in your early twenties, but you had always sensed that your grandmother was mad, that this small immigrant woman with her broken English and violent screaming spells was someone to be kept at arm's length. Even as the mourners drifted in and out of the house, you went about your ten-year-old-boy's business, and when the rabbi put his hand on your shoulder and said it would be all right for you to go off and play in your Little League game that evening, you went up to your room, put on your baseball uniform, and ran out of the house.

Eleven years later, the death of your mother's mother was a different story. You were grown then, the bolt of lightning that had killed your friend when you were fourteen had taught you that the world was capricious and unstable, that the future can be stolen from us at any moment, that the sky is full of lightning bolts that can crash down and kill the young as well as the old, and always, always, the lightning strikes when we are least expecting it. This was the grandmother you cared about, the prim and slightly nervous woman you loved, the one who stayed with you often and was a consistent presence in your life, and now that you are thinking about her death, the nature of her death, which was slow and dreadful and anguishing to watch, you realize that all the other deaths in your family have been sudden, a series of lightning bolts similar to the one that killed your friend: your father's mother (heart attack, dead within hours), your father's father (shot and killed before you knew him), your father (heart attack, dead within seconds), your mother (heart attack, dead within minutes), and even your mother's father, whose death was not instantaneous, who made it to eighty-five in good health and then, after a swift decline of two or three weeks, died of pneumonia, which is to say, died of old age—a death to be envied, you feel, full-bore life into your ninth decade and then, rather than electrocution by lightning bolt, a chance to absorb the fact that you are on your way out, a chance to reflect for a while, and then you go to sleep and float off into the land of nothingness. Your grandmother didn't float anywhere. For two years she was dragged over a bed of nails, and when she died at seventy-three, there was little of anything left of her. Amyotrophic lateral sclerosis, commonly known as Lou Gehrig's disease. You have seen people's bodies consumed by the autocannibalism of virulent cancer, have watched the gradual strangulation of others by emphysema, but ALS is no less ravaging or cruel, and once you have been diagnosed with it, there is no hope, no remedy, nothing in front of you but a prolonged march toward disintegration and death. Your bones melt. The skeleton inside your skin turns to putty, and one by one your organs fail. What made your grandmother's case particularly hard to bear was that the first symptoms appeared in her throat, and her speech functions were attacked before anything else: larynx, tongue, esophagus. One day, out of nowhere, she found it difficult to pronounce her words clearly, the syllables came out slurred, slightly off. A month or two later, they were alarmingly off. Several months after that, rattles of phlegm occluding her sentences, choked-off gurglings, the humiliations of impairment, and when no New York doctor could figure out what was wrong with her, your mother took her to the Mayo Clinic for a full workup. The men in Minnesota were the ones who pronounced her death sentence, and before long her speech had become unintelligible. She was forced to communicate in writing after that, carrying a little pencil and a pad of paper wherever she went, though for the time being the rest of her seemed well, she could still walk, still take part in the life around her, but as the months passed and the musculature of her throat continued to atrophy, swallowing became problematic, eating and drinking became a permanent trial, and in the end the rest of her body began to betray her as well. For the first week or two in the hospital, she still had the use of her arms and hands, could still use the pencil and pad to communicate, even though her handwriting had deteriorated badly, and then she came under the watch of a private nurse named Miss Moran (short and efficient, a rictus of perpetual false cheer glued onto her face), who kept the pad and pencil from your grandmother, and the more your grandmother howled in protest, the longer that pad was kept from her. Once you and your mother got wind of what was going on, Moran was fired, but the battle your grandmother had fought with the sadistic nurse had depleted whatever strength she had left. The gentle, self-effacing woman who had read you Maupassant stories when you were ill, who had taken you to shows at Radio City Music Hall, who had treated you to ice cream sundaes and lunches at Schrafft's was dying in Doctors Hospital on the Upper East Side of Manhattan, and not long after she became too weak to hold the pencil anymore, she lost her mind. Whatever force she still had in her was subsumed by rage, a demented anger that made her unrecognizable and expressed itself in constant howls, the throttled, dammed-up howls of a helpless, immobilized person struggling not to drown in a puddle of her own sputum. Born in Minsk, 1895. Died in New York, 1968. *The end of life is bitter* (Joseph Joubert, 1814).

Things were the way they were, and you never stopped to question them. There were public schools and Catholic schools in your town, and because you were not Catholic, you attended the public schools, which were considered to be good schools, at least by the standards that were used to measure such things at the time, and according to what your mother later told you, it was for this reason that your family had moved to the house on Irving Avenue in the months before you were scheduled to begin kindergarten. You have nothing to compare your experience with, but in the thirteen years you spent in that system, the first seven at Marshall School (K–6), the next three at South Orange Junior High School (7–9), and the last three at Columbia High School in Maplewood (10–12), you had some good teachers and some mediocre teachers, a handful of exceptional and inspiring teachers and a handful of lousy and incompetent teachers, and your fellow students ranged from the brilliant to the average to the semi-moronic. Such is the case with all public schools. Everyone who lives in the district can go for free, and because you grew up in a time before the advent of special education, before separate schools had been established to accommodate children with so-called problems, a number of your classmates were physically handicapped. No one in a wheelchair that you can remember, but you can still see the hunchbacked boy with the twisted body, the girl who was missing an arm (a fingerless stump jutting from her shoulder), the drooling boy who slobbered down the front of his shirt, and the girl who was scarcely taller than a midget. Looking back on it now, you feel that these people were an essential part of your education, that without their presence in your life your understanding of what it means to be human would have been impoverished, lacking all depth and compassion, all insight into the metaphysics of pain and adversity, for those children were the heroic ones, the ones who had to work ten times harder than any of the others to find a place for themselves. If you had lived only among the physically blessed, the children like yourself who took your well-formed bodies for granted, how would you have ever learned what heroism was? One of your friends from those early years was a plump, nonathletic boy with glasses and a homely, chinless sort of face, but he was much loved by the other boys for his sharp wit and humor, his prowess at math, and what struck you then as an uncommon generosity of spirit. He had a bedridden younger brother, a boy suffering from a disease that had stunted his growth and left him with brittle bones, bones that broke from the slightest contact with hard surfaces, bones that broke for no reason at all, and you can remember visiting your friend's house after school on several occasions and going in to see his brother, who was just a year or two younger than you were, lying in a hospital bed rigged with pulleys and wires, his legs in plaster casts, with his large head and impossibly pale skin, and you could hardly open your mouth in that room, you felt nervous, perhaps a bit scared, but the brother was a nice kid, friendly and affable and bright, and it always struck you as absurd, altogether outrageous that he should be lying in that bed, and every time you saw him you wondered what idiot god had decreed that he should be locked inside that body and not you. Your friend was devoted to him, they were as close to each other as any brothers you have ever known, and they shared a private, two-person world, a secret universe dominated by a mutual obsession with the fantasy baseball game they played, a board game with dice, cards, complex rules, and elaborate statistics, meticulously keeping records of every game they played, which evolved into entire seasons of games, every month or two another season, season after season of imaginary games as the years rolled on. How perfectly right, you realize now, that it should have been this friend of yours who called you one evening in the winter of 1957–58, not long after the Dodgers had announced their move from Brooklyn to Los Angeles, to tell you that Roy Campanella, the All-Star catcher, had been in a car accident, an accident so terrible that even if he pulled through, he would be paralyzed for the rest of his life. Your friend was weeping into the phone.

February twenty-third: the thirtieth anniversary of the day you met your wife, the thirtieth anniversary of the first night you spent together. The two of you leave your house in the late afternoon, cross the Brooklyn Bridge, and check into a hotel in lower Manhattan. A bit of an indulgence, perhaps, but you don't want these twenty-four hours to slip by without doing something to mark the occasion, and because the idea of throwing a party never came up (why would a couple want to celebrate its longevity in front of others?), you and your wife eat dinner alone in the hotel restaurant. Afterward, you take the elevator to the ninth floor and enter your room, where you polish off a bottle of champagne together, forgetting to turn on the radio, forgetting to turn on the television to investigate the four thousand movies that are available to you, and as you drink the champagne you talk to each other, for several hours you do nothing but talk, not about the past and the thirty years that are behind you but about the present, about your daughter and your wife's mother, about the work you are both engaged in now, about any number of things both pertinent and trivial, and in that respect this evening is no different from any other evening of your marriage, since the two of you have always talked, that is what defines you somehow, and for all these years you have been living inside the long, uninterrupted conversation that started the day you met. Outside, another cold winter night, another burst of freezing rain lashing against the windows, but you are in bed with your wife now, and the hotel bed is warm, the sheets are smooth and comfortable, and the pillows are positively gigantic.

Numerous crushes and flirtations, but only two big loves in your early life, the cataclysms of your mid-teens and late teens, both of which were disasters, followed by your first marriage, which ended in disaster as well. Starting in 1962, when you fell for the beautiful English girl in your tenth-grade English class, you seemed to have a special talent for chasing after the wrong person, for wanting what you couldn't have, for giving your heart to girls who couldn't or wouldn't love you back. Occasional interest in your mind, flashes of interest in your body, but none whatsoever in your heart. Half-crazy girls, both of them ravishing and self-destructive and deeply exciting to you, but you understood almost nothing about them. You invented them. You used them as fictive embodiments of your own desires, ignoring their problems and personal histories, failing to grasp who they were outside of your own imagination, and yet the more they eluded you, the more passionately you longed for them. The one in high school went on a secret hunger strike and wound up in the hospital. The word *anorexia* was not in your vocabulary at the time, and so you thought cancer or leukemia (which had killed her mother a few years earlier), for how else to account for the dwindling of her once lovely body, the horrid emaciation, and you remember trying to visit her in the hospital and being turned away, every afternoon turned away, out of your mind with love, with fear, but in the end she was not made for boys, and even though she drifted back into your life a couple of times when you were in your early twenties (ending with the crab louse debacle), she was essentially a girl made for other girls, and therefore you never had a chance with her. The second story began in the winter of your first year of college, when you fell for another unstable girl who both wanted you and didn't want you, and the more she didn't want you, the more ardently you pursued her. A sick troubadour and his inconstant lady, and even after she slashed her wrists in a halfhearted suicide attempt a few months later, you went on loving her, the one with the white bandages and the fetching, crooked smile, and then, after the bandages were removed, you made her pregnant, the condom you were using broke, and you spent every penny you had to pay for an abortion. A brutal memory, another one of the things that still keep you awake at night, and while you are certain the two of you made the correct decision not to have the baby (parents at nineteen and twenty, a grotesque thought), you are tormented by the memory of that unborn child. You always imagined it would be a girl, a girl with red hair, a wondrous firecracker of a girl, and it pains you to realize that she would be forty-three years old now, which means that in all probability you would have become a grandfather some time ago, perhaps a long time ago. If you had let her live.

In the light of your past failures, your misjudgments, your inability to understand yourself and others, your impulsive and erratic decisions, your blundering approach to matters of the heart, it seems curious that you should have wound up in a marriage that has lasted this long. You have tried to figure out the reasons for this unexpected reversal of fortune, but you have never been able to come up with an answer. You ran into a stranger one night and fell in love with her—and she fell in love with you. You didn't deserve it, but neither did you not deserve it. It just happened, and nothing can account for what happened to you except luck.

From the very start, everything was different with her. Not a figment this time, not some projection of your inner fancy, but a real person, and she imposed her reality on you the moment the two of you began to talk, which was one moment after the single acquaintance you had in common introduced you to each other in the lobby of the 92nd Street Y following a poetry reading, and because she was neither coy nor elusive, because she looked you in the eye and asserted herself as a wholly grounded presence, there was no way for you to turn her into something she was not—no way to invent her, as you had done with other women in the past, since she had already invented herself. Beautiful, yes, without question sublimely beautiful, a lean six-foot blonde with long, magnificent legs and the tiny wrists of a four-year-old, the biggest little person you had ever seen, or perhaps the littlest big person, and yet you were not looking at some remote object of female splendor, you were engaged in talking to a living, breathing human subject. Subject, not object, and therefore no delusions permitted. No deceptions possible. Intelligence is the one human quality that cannot be faked, and once your eyes had adjusted to the dazzle of her beauty, you understood that this was a brilliant woman, one of the best minds you had ever met.

Little by little, as you came to know her better in the weeks that followed, you discovered that you saw eye to eye on nearly everything of any importance. Your politics were the same, most of the books you cared about were the same books, and you had similar attitudes about what you wanted out of life: love, work, and children—with money and possessions far down on the list. Much to your relief, your personalities were nothing alike. She laughed more than you did, she was freer and more outgoing than you were, she was warmer than you were, and yet, all the way down at the bottom, at the nethermost point where you were joined together, you felt that you had met another version of yourself—but one that was more fully evolved than you were, better able to express what you kept bottled up inside you, a saner being. You adored her, and for the first time in your life, the person you adored adored you back. You came from entirely different worlds, a young Lutheran girl from Minnesota and a not so young Jew from New York, but just two and a half months after your chance encounter on February twenty-third thirty years ago, you decided to move in together. Until then, every decision you had made about women had been a wrong decision—but not this one.

She was a graduate student and a poet, and in the first five years you were together you watched her finish up her course work, study for and pass her oral exams, and then go through the arduous slog of writing her dissertation (on language and identity in Dickens). She published one book of poetry during that time, and because money was scarce in the early days of your marriage, she worked at several different jobs, editing a three-volume anthology published by Zone Books for one thing, secretly rewriting someone's doctoral dissertation on Jacques Lacan for another, and also teaching, most of all teaching. The first class was for low-level employees at an insurance company, ambitious young workers who wanted to improve their chances for promotion by taking an intensive course in English grammar and expository writing. Twice a week, your wife came home with stories about her students, some of them entertaining, some of them rather poignant, but the one you remember best concerns a howler that appeared on the final exam. Midway through the semester, your wife had given a lecture on various figures of speech, among them the concept of euphemism. By way of example, she had cited *pass away* as a euphemism for *die*. On the final exam, she asked the members of the class to give a definition of the word *euphemism*, and one vaguely attentive but challenged student answered: "Euphemism means *to die*." After the insurance company, she moved on to Queens College, where she worked as an adjunct for three years, a grinding, badly paid job, two courses per semester with classes in remedial English and English composition, twenty-five students per class, fifty papers a week to correct, three private conferences with each student every semester, a two-hour trip from Cobble Hill to Flushing that began at six in the morning and entailed two subways and a bus, then another two-hour trip in the opposite direction, all for a salary of eight thousand dollars a year with no benefits. The long days wore her out, not just because of the work and the travel but also because of the hours spent under the fluorescent lights at Queens, the rapidly flickering lights that can induce headaches in people who suffer from migraine, and because your wife had been saddled with that condition since childhood, it was the rare evening when she didn't walk through the door with dark circles under her eyes and a head bursting with pain. Her dissertation was advancing slowly, the weekly schedule was too fragmented for concentrated periods of research and writing, but suddenly your finances began to improve somewhat, enough for you to persuade her to quit the teaching job at any rate, and once she was free, she knocked off the rest of her Dickens thesis in six months. The bigger question was why she was still so determined to finish. Graduate school had made sense in the beginning: a single woman needs a job, especially if that woman comes from a family with no money, and even though her ambition was to write, she couldn't count on writing to sustain her, and therefore she would become a professor. But things were different now. She was married, her money situation was becoming less and less precarious, she was no longer planning to look for an academic job, and still she battled on until she had earned her doctorate. Again and again, you asked her why it was so important to her, and the various answers she gave you all go straight to the heart of who she was then, who she still is today. First: because she couldn't bring herself to quit something she had started. A question of stubbornness and pride. Second: because she was a woman. It was all very well that you had bailed out of graduate school after one year, you were a man, and men control the world, but a woman who wears the badge of an advanced degree will gain some respect in that man's world, will not be looked down upon as much as a woman who does not have that badge. Third: because she loved it. The hard work and discipline of intense study had improved her mind, had made her a better and more subtle thinker, and even if most of her time would be spent writing novels in the future (she had already started her first), she had no intention of abandoning her intellectual life once she had her Ph.D. These were discussions you had with her more than twenty-five years ago, but it was as if she had already begun to squint into the future and see the outlines of what lay in front of her. Since then: five published novels and a sixth in the works, but also four books of nonfiction, for the most part essays, dozens of essays on an enormous range of subjects: literature, art, culture, politics, films, daily life, fashion, neuroscience, psychoanalysis, the philosophy of perception, and the phenomenology of memory. In 1978, she was one of a hundred students who entered the graduate English program at Columbia. Seven years later, she was one of only three who had made it all the way to the end.

By marrying your wife, you married into her family as well, and because her parents still lived in the house where she had grown up, another country was gradually absorbed into your bloodstream: Minnesota, the northernmost province in the rural kingdom of the Upper Midwest. Not the flat world you'd imagined it would be, but an undulating land of small peaks and dipping curves, no mountains or hilly extrusions and yet clouds in the far distance that simulate mountains and hills, an illusory bulk, a mass of vaporous white to soften the monotony of mile after mile of undulating land, and on days when there are no clouds, the alfalfa fields that stretch all the way to the horizon, a low and distant horizon over-arched by an enormous, never-ending sky, a sky so large that it comes all the way down to your toes. The coldest winters on earth, followed by broiling, humid summers, torrid heat bearing down on you with millions of mosquitoes, so many mosquitoes that T-shirts are sold bearing pictures of those homicidal dive-bombers with the legend MINNESOTA—THE STATE BIRD. The first time you went out there, for a two-month stay in the summer of 1981, you were writing the preface to your anthology of twentieth-century French poetry, a long-ish piece that ran to forty-something pages, and because your future wife's parents were out of town during your visit, you worked in your future father-in-law's office on the St. Olaf College campus, cranking out paragraphs about Apollinaire, Reverdy, and Breton in a room decorated with pictures of Viking helmets, driving each morning to the mostly deserted campus, which suddenly came to life one week when the college rented out some of its buildings to the annual Conference of Christian Coaches, and how you enjoyed seeing those coaches walk by when you parked your car in the morning, dozens of nearly identical-looking men with their crew cuts, potbellies, and Bermuda shorts, and then on to your room in the Norwegian Department, where you would write another couple of pages about French poets. You were in Northfield, which advertised itself as "The Home of Cows, Colleges, and Contentment," a town of about eight thousand people, best known as the place where Jesse James and his gang met their end during an attempted holdup (the bullet holes are still in the walls of the bank on Division Street), but your favorite spot quickly became the Malt-O-Meal factory on Highway 19, with its tall smokestacks pouring out white clouds of the nut-scented grain used in the recipe for that tawny, farina-textured breakfast cereal, located midway between your in-laws' house and the center of town, just a few hundred yards before the railroad tracks you stopped in front of with your wife one afternoon that summer as a slowly moving train passed by, the longest train you have ever seen, somewhere between one and two hundred freight cars, but you didn't have time to count them because you and your then future wife were talking, chiefly about the apartment you would be looking for when you returned to New York, and that was when the question of marriage first came up between you, not just living together under the same roof but bound by matrimony as well, that was what she wanted, that was what she insisted upon, and even though you had decided never to marry again, you said of course, you would gladly marry her if that was what she wanted, for you had loved her long enough by then to know that whatever she wanted was precisely what you wanted as well. That was why you paid such close attention to everything around you that summer, because this was the country where she had spent her girlhood and early womanhood, and by studying the details of that landscape you felt you would come to know her better, understand her better, and one by one, as you came to know her mother and father and three younger sisters, you began to acquire an understanding of her family as well, which also helped you understand her better, to feel the solidity of the ground she walked on, for this was a solid family, nothing like the fractured, provisional family you yourself had grown up in, and it wasn't long before you became one of them, for this, to your everlasting good fortune, was now your family, too.

Then came the winter visits, the turn-of-the-year homecomings, a week to ten days in a frozen world of silent air, of windborne daggers piercing your body, of looking at the thermometer through the kitchen window in the morning and seeing the red mercury stuck at twenty below zero Fahrenheit, thirty below zero, temperatures so inhospitable to human life you have often wondered how anyone could live in such a place, your head filled with images of Sioux families wrapped from head to toe in buffalo pelts, pioneer families freezing to death on the tundralike prairie. No cold like this cold, an impossible cold that stuns the muscles in your face the instant you step outdoors, that pummels your skin, puckers your skin, that coagulates the blood in your veins, and yet once, not many years ago, the entire family went out into the dark to look at the northern lights, you saw them only that one time, unforgettable, unimaginable—standing in the cold and gazing up at an electric green sky, a sky flashing green against the black wall of night, nothing you have witnessed has ever come close to the hectic grandeur of that spectacle. On other nights, the clear nights without clouds, a sky crammed with stars, packed full from horizon to horizon, more stars than you have seen anywhere else, so many stars that they merge into dense liquid pools, a porridge of whiteness overhead, and the white mornings that follow, the white afternoons, the snow, the snow that falls endlessly all around you, up to your knees, up to your waist, growing like the sunflower that shot past your head in your mother's garden when you were a boy, more snow than you have seen anywhere else, and suddenly you are reliving a moment from the mid-nineties, when you and your wife and daughter had made the annual Christmas pilgrimage to Minnesota, and there you are behind the wheel on the night of a blizzard, driving from the house of one of your wife's sisters in Minneapolis to her parents' house in Northfield, just under forty miles away. Sitting in the backseat are three generations of women (your mother-in-law, wife, and daughter), and up front with you, sitting in the passenger seat to your right, is your father-in-law, a man who has treated you with kindness during the years of your marriage to his oldest daughter, even if in many ways he is a remote and shut-down person, much as your own father was, both men having endured rough and impoverished childhoods, and in your father-in-law's case there was the added ordeal of having served as a young foot soldier in World War II (the Battle of Luzon, the Philippines, the jungles of New Guinea), but you are a lifelong expert in the art of communicating with shut-down men, and if your father-in-law sometimes resembles your father, you feel that there is a larger reservoir of warmth and tenderness in him, that he is more knowable than your father ever was, more fully a member of the human race. You are forty-six or forty-seven years old, in excellent physical condition, still youthful in the middle of your middle age, and because you are still known as a *good driver*, the female contingent in the backseat has absolute faith in your ability to deliver them safely to the house in Northfield, and because they trust you, they are not alarmed by the potential dangers of the storm. All during the ride home, in fact, the three of them engage in animated talk on any number of subjects, acting as if it were a mild evening at the height of summer, but the instant you start the car and pull away from your sister-in-law's house, both you and your father-in-law know that you are in for a hellish ride, that weather conditions are bad to the point of impossible. Once you reach the highway and begin traveling south on I-35, the snow is lashing onto the windshield, and although the wipers are working at full speed, you can see almost nothing, since the snow starts gathering on the glass again the instant the wipers complete their arc. There are no overhead lamps on the highway, but the oncoming headlights of the cars traveling toward you in the opposite lane illuminate the snow as it falls onto the windshield, so that what you are seeing is no longer snow but a shower of small, blinding lights. Worst of all, the road is slick, as smooth and icy as a skating pond, and to go more than ten or fifteen miles an hour would rob the tires of their traction and render the brakes useless. Every fifty or a hundred yards, both to your left and to your right, you pass another car that has skidded off the road, lying half-overturned in a mountainous snowbank or drift. Your father-in-law, who has lived in Minnesota all his life, is all too familiar with the hazards of driving in a storm like this one, and he is entirely with you as you inch the car along through the night, sitting in the navigator's seat and peering into the spangled clouds of snow that continue to pour down onto the windshield, warning you of upcoming curves, keeping you calm and focused, driving with you in his head, in the muscles of his body, and so it is that you finally make it to the house in Northfield, you and the old soldier in front, the women in back, a two-hour trek instead of the customary thirty or forty minutes, and when the five of you enter the house, the women are still talking and laughing, but your father-in-law, who knows what a trial this has been on your nerves, since it has been a trial on his nerves as well, pats you on the back and gives you a little wink. Fifty years after he hung up his uniform, the sergeant has saluted you.

Christmas dinner in Northfield, Minnesota, every year from 1981 until your father-in-law's death in 2004, after which the family house was sold, your mother-in-law moved to an apartment, and the tradition was altered to fit the new circumstances. But for close to a quarter century the meal was formalized down to the last detail, not one element different from the year before, and the table you first sat down to in 1981, which consisted of just seven people—your mother-in-law and father-in-law, your wife, her three sisters, and yourself—gradually expanded as one year melted into another and your wife's younger sisters married and began having children of their own, so by the end of that quarter-century run, nineteen people were sitting around the table, including the very old and the old, the young and the very young. It is important to note that Christmas was celebrated on the night of the twenty-fourth, not on the morning and afternoon of the twenty-fifth, for even though your wife's family lived in the American heartland, they were and are a Scandinavian family as well, a Norwegian family, and all Christmas protocols followed the conventions from that part of the world rather than this one. Your mother-in-law, born in the southernmost town of Norway in 1923, did not move across the Atlantic until she was thirty, and although her English is fluent, she continues to speak this second tongue with a pronounced Norwegian accent. She lived through the war and the German occupation as a young woman, was put in prison for nine days after participating in an early protest march against the Nazis when she was seventeen (if it had happened later in the war, she says, she would have been sent to a camp), and both of her older brothers were active members of the underground (one of them, after his cell was broken, skied to Sweden in order to escape the Gestapo). Your mother-in-law is an intelligent, well-read person, someone you greatly admire and feel much affection for, but her occasional struggles with the English language and American geography have produced some strange moments, none more hilarious, perhaps, than the night fifteen or sixteen years ago when the plane she and her husband were taking to Boston could not land because the airport was fogged in and consequently had to be rerouted to Albany, New York, and once they made it to Albany she called your wife and announced over the telephone: "We're in Albania! We're spending the night in Albania!" As for your father-in-law, he too was thoroughly Norwegian, even though he was a third-generation American, born in Cannon Falls, Minnesota, in 1922, the last of the nineteenth-century prairie children, a farm boy raised in a log house without electricity or indoor plumbing, and the rural community where he lived was so isolated, so unanimously populated by Norwegian immigrants and their descendents, that much of his early life was transacted in Norwegian rather than in English, so that he retained an accent throughout his adulthood and old age: not a heavy accent like your mother-in-law's but a soft musical brogue, an American English spoken in a way you have never heard from anyone else and which you always found highly pleasing to the ear. After the long interruption of the war, he finished college on the G.I. Bill, continued his studies through graduate school and a Fulbright year at the University of Oslo (where he and your mother-in-law met), and wound up as a professor of Norwegian language and literature. Your wife grew up in a Norwegian household, then, even if it happened to be located in Minnesota, and Christmas dinner was therefore strictly and resolutely Norwegian as well. In effect, it was a duplication of the Christmas dinners your mother-in-law ate with her own family as a child in southern Norway back in the 1920s and '30s, a time far removed from our current age of opulence and plenty, of supermarkets stocked with two hundred kinds of breakfast cereal and eighty-four flavors of ice cream. The meal never varied, and in twenty-three years not one dish was ever added to the menu or subtracted from it. Not turkey or goose or ham, as one might suppose for the main course, but pork ribs, covered lightly in salt and pepper, baked in the oven, and served without sauce or condiments. Accompanied by boiled potatoes, cauliflower, red cabbage, Brussels sprouts, carrots, lingonberries, and rice pudding for desert. No meal could be simpler than this one, more defiantly at odds with contemporary American notions about what constitutes acceptable holiday fare, and yet when you polled the youngest of your nieces and nephews a couple of years ago (the tradition still carries on in New York), asking them if they liked Christmas dinner as it was or if they would prefer to see some changes, they all cried out: "No changes!" This is food as ritual, as continuity, as family cohesion—a symbolic anchor to prevent you from drifting out to sea. Such is the tribe you have married into. When she was around fifteen, your witty daughter came up with a new term to describe her background: Jew-wegian. You doubt there are many people who can lay claim to that particular brand of hyphenated identity, but this is America, after all, and yes, you and your wife are the parents of a Jew-wegian.

The foods you loved as boy, from the time of your earliest memories to the threshold of puberty, and you wonder now how many thousands of forkfuls and spoonfuls went into you, how many bites and swallows, how many small sips and grand gulps, beginning with the myriad fruit juices you drank at various times during the day, orange juice in the morning, but also apple juice and grapefruit juice and tomato juice and pineapple juice, pineapple juice in a glass but also pineapple juice frozen in ice cube trays during the summer, which you and your sister referred to as "pineapple chunks," along with the soft drinks you downed whenever you were permitted to (Coca-Cola, root beer, ginger ale, 7 Up, Orange Crush), and the milkshakes you adored, especially chocolate, but sometimes vanilla for a change of pace, or a combination of the two known as a black-and-white, and then, in the summer, the delirium of the root beer float, traditionally made with vanilla ice cream, but for you even more delicious if the flavor of the ice cream was coffee. On any given morning, you would begin with a first course of cold cereal (Corn Flakes, Rice Krispies, Shredded Wheat, Puffed Wheat, Puffed Rice, Cheerios—whatever happened to be in the kitchen cupboard), which you would pour into a bowl, douse with milk, and then coat with a tablespoon (or two tablespoons) of white refined sugar.

Followed by a serving of eggs (scrambled mostly, but occasionally fried or soft-boiled) and two pieces of buttered toast (white, whole wheat, or rye), often accompanied by bacon, ham, or sausage, or else a platter of French toast (with maple syrup), or, rarely, but always most coveted, a stack of pancakes (also with maple syrup). Several hours later, lunch meats piled between two slices of bread, ham or salami, corned beef or bologna, sometimes ham and American cheese together, sometimes American cheese alone, or else one of your mother's dependable tuna fish sandwiches. On cold days, cold winter days like this one, the sandwich was often preceded by a bowl of soup, which always came out of cans in the early fifties, your favorites being Campbell's chicken noodle and Campbell's tomato, which no doubt was the case with every other American child back then as well. Hamburgers and hot dogs, french fries and potato chips: once-a-week delicacies in the local malt shop known as the Cricklewood, where you and your school friends would eat lunch together every Thursday. (Your grammar school did not have a cafeteria. Everyone would go home for lunch, but starting when you were nine or ten, your mother and the mothers of your friends allowed you this treat: hamburgers and/or hot dogs at the Cricklewood every Thursday, which cost all of twenty-five or thirty cents.) The evening meal, interchangeably referred to as dinner or supper, was best if the main dish was lamb chops, but roast beef ran a close second, followed, in no particular order, by fried chicken, roast chicken, beef stew, pot roast, spaghetti and meatballs, sautéed liver, and fried fish fillets smothered in ketchup. Potatoes were a constant, and however they were served (primarily baked or mashed), they never failed to offer profound satisfaction. Corn on the cob surpassed all other vegetables, but that delight was confined to the last months of summer, and therefore you happily wolfed down the peas or peas and carrots or green beans or beets you found on your plate. Popcorn, pistachio nuts, peanuts, marshmallows, piles of saltines smeared with grape jelly, and the frozen foods that began appearing late in your childhood, in particular chicken pot pie and Sara Lee's pound cake. You have all but lost your taste for sweets at this point in your life, but when you look back on the distant days of your boyhood, you are staggered by how many sugary things you longed for and devoured. Ice cream most of all, for which you seemed to have an insatiable appetite, whether served up plain in a bowl or covered in chocolate sauce, whether presented in the form of a sundae or a float, ice cream on a stick (as in Good Humor bars and Creamsicles) as well as ice cream lurking inside spheres (Bon Bons), rectangles (Eskimo Pies), and domes (Baked Alaska). Ice cream was the tobacco of your youth, the addiction that slinked its way into your soul and endlessly seduced you with its charms, but you were also a pushover for cake (chocolate layer! angel food!) and every variety of cookie, from Vanilla Fingers to Burry's Double Dip Chocolate, from Fig Newtons to Mallomars, from Oreos to Social Tea Biscuits, not to mention the hundreds if not thousands of candy bars you consumed before the age of twelve: Milky Ways, Three Musketeers, Chunkys,

Charleston Chews, York Mints, Junior Mints, Mars bars, Snickers bars, Baby Ruths, Milk Duds, Chuckles, Goobers, Dots, Jujubes, Sugar Daddys, and God knows what else. How is it possible that you managed to stay thin during the years when you were ingesting all this sugar, that your body somehow continued to grow upward rather than outward as you veered toward adolescence? Thankfully, all that is behind you now, but every now and then, perhaps once every two or three years, while you are killing time in an airport before a long-distance flight (for some reason, this happens only in airports), if you should wander into the magazine shop to look for a newspaper, an ancient longing will suddenly take hold of you, and then you will cast your eyes down at the sweets on display below the cash register, and if they happen to have Chuckles in stock, you will buy them. Within ten minutes, all five of the jellied candies will be gone. Red, yellow, green, orange, and black.

Joubert: *The end of life is bitter.* Less than a year after writing those words, at the age of sixty-one, which must have seemed considerably older in 1815 than it does today, he jotted down a different and far more challenging formulation about the end of life: *One must die lovable (if one can).* You are moved by this sentence, especially by the words in parentheses, which demonstrate a rare sensitivity of spirit, you feel, a hard-won understanding of how difficult it is to be lovable, especially for someone who is old, who is sinking into decrepitude and must be cared for by others. *If one can.* There is probably no greater human achievement than to be lovable at the end, whether that end is bitter or not. Fouling the deathbed with piss and shit and drool. We are all going there, you tell yourself, and the question is to what degree a person can remain human while hanging on in a state of helplessness and degradation. You cannot predict what will happen when the day comes for you to crawl into bed for the last time, but if you are not taken suddenly, as both of your parents were, you want to be lovable. *If you can.*

You mustn't neglect to mention that you nearly choked to death on a fish bone in 1971 or that you narrowly escaped killing yourself in a dark hallway one night in 2006 when you smashed your forehead into a low door frame, stumbled backward, and then, trying to regain your balance, pitched forward, snagged your foot on the sill, and went flying face-first onto the floor of the apartment you had entered, the top of your head landing within inches of a thick table leg. Every day, in every country around the world, people die from falls like that one. Your friend's uncle, for example, the same man you wrote about nineteen years ago (*The Red Notebook*, Story No. 3), who survived gunshot wounds and multiple dangers as a partisan resistance fighter against the Nazis in World War II, a young man who managed to escape certain death and/or mutilation with dumbfounding regularity, and then, having moved to Chicago after the war, living in the tranquility of peacetime America, far from the battlefields and flying bullets and exploding land mines of his youth, awoke one night to go to the bathroom, tripped over a piece of furniture in the darkened living room, and died when his head smashed into a thick table leg. An absurd death, a nonsensical death, a death that could have been yours five years ago if your head had landed just a few inches to the left, and when you think about the ridiculous ways in which people can meet their end—tumbling down flights of stairs, slipping off ladders, accidentally drowning, being run over by cars, shot by stray bullets, electrocuted by radios that fall into bathtubs—you can only conclude that every life is marked by a number of close calls, that everyone who manages to reach the age you have come to now has already wriggled out of a number of potentially absurd, nonsensical deaths. All in the course of what you would call *ordinary life*. Needless to say, millions of others have confronted far worse, have not had the luxury of leading an ordinary life, soldiers in combat, for example, civilian casualties in wars, the murdered victims of totalitarian governments, and the countless many who have perished in natural disasters: floods, earthquakes, typhoons, epidemics. But even those who manage to survive catastrophe are no less prey to the whims of daily existence than those of us who have been spared such horrors—as with your friend's uncle, who eluded death in battle and died one night in a Chicago apartment on his way to the bathroom. In 1971, the fish bone lodged itself at the base of your throat. You were eating what you thought was a fillet of halibut, and for that reason you were not worried about encountering any bones, but suddenly you could no longer swallow without pain, something was *in there,* and none of the traditional remedies did the least bit of good: drinking water, eating bread, trying to pull the bone out with your fingers. The bone had traveled too far down your throat, and it was long enough and thick enough to have pierced the skin on both sides, and each time you made another attempt to cough it up, your saliva was mixed with blood. It was April or May, you had been living in Paris for two or two and a half months, and when it became clear that you would not be able to get rid of the bone yourself, you and your girlfriend left your apartment on the rue Jacques Mawas and walked to the nearest medical facility in the neighborhood, l'Hôpital Boucicaut. It was eight or nine o'clock in the evening, and the nurses had no idea what to do with you. They squirted a liquid numbing agent down your throat, they chatted with you, they laughed, but the stuck bone was inaccessible and therefore could not be extracted. Finally, at around eleven o'clock, the nighttime emergency doctor came on duty, a young man by the name of Meyer, yet one more Israelite in this neighborhood once inhabited by the blind piano tuner, and lo and behold, this young doctor, who couldn't have been more than four or five years older than you were, turned out to be an ear, nose, and throat specialist. After you spat up some blood for him during the preliminary examination, he told you to follow him through the courtyard to his private office in another one of the hospital's pavilions. You sat down in a chair, he sat down in a chair, and then he opened a large leather case filled with thirty or forty sets of tweezers, an impressive array of shining silver instruments, tweezers of every possible size and configuration, some with straight ends, some with curved ends, some with hooked ends, some with twisting ends, some with looping ends, some short and some long, some so intricate and bizarre-looking that you could not imagine how such things could travel down a person's throat. He told you to open your mouth, and one by one he gently guided various sets of tweezers into and down your gullet—so far down that you gagged and spat up more blood each time he pulled another one out. Patience, he said to you, patience, we're going to get it, and then, on the fifteenth try, using one of the largest pairs of tweezers, the grandfather pair with a grotesquely exaggerated scimitar of a hook at the end, he finally got a purchase on the bone, clamped down on it, wiggled it back and forth to free the points that were embedded in your flesh, and slowly lifted it up through the tunnel of your throat and out into the open air. He looked both pleased and astonished. Pleased by his success, but astonished by the size of the bone, which was a good three or four inches long. You were astonished as well. How could you have swallowed such a massive object? you asked yourself. It reminded you of an Eskimo sewing needle, a whalebone corset stay, a poison dart. "You're lucky," Dr. Meyer said, still looking at the bone as he held it up in front of your face. "This one easily could have killed you."

No snow of any significance since the night of February first, but a frigid month with little sun, much rain, much wind, hunkered down in your room every day writing this journal, this journey through winter, and now into March, still cold, still as cold as the winter cold of January and February, and yet every morning you go outside to peruse the garden now, looking for a sign of color, the smallest tip of a crocus leaf jutting from the ground, the first dab of yellow on the forsythia bush, but nothing to report so far, spring will be coming late this year, and you wonder how many more weeks will go by before you can begin searching for your first robin.

The dancers saved you. They are the ones who brought you back to life that evening in December 1978, who made it possible for you to experience *the scalding, epiphanic moment of clarity that pushed you through a crack in the universe* and allowed you to begin again. Bodies in motion, bodies in space, bodies leaping and twisting through empty, unimpeded air, eight dancers in a high school gym in Manhattan, four men and four women, all of them young, eight dancers in their early twenties, and you sitting in the bleachers with a dozen or so acquaintances of the choreographer's to watch an open rehearsal of her new piece. You had been invited by David Reed, a painter you met on the student ship that took you to Europe in 1965, now your oldest friend in New York, who had asked you to come because he was romantically involved with the choreographer, Nina W., a woman you did not know well and whose affair with David did not last long, but, if you are not distorting the facts, you believe she had started out as a dancer in Merce Cunningham's troupe, and now that she had turned her energies to choreography, her work bore some resemblance to Cunningham's: muscular, spontaneous, unpredictable. It was the darkest moment of your life. You were thirty-one years old, your first marriage had just cracked apart, you had an eighteen-month-old son and no regular job, no money to speak of, grinding out your meager, inadequate living as a freelance translator, author of three small books of poetry with at most one hundred readers in the world, padding your pittance of an income by writing critical pieces for *Harper's*, the *New York Review of Books*, and other magazines, and apart from a pseudonymous detective novel you had written the previous summer in an effort to generate some cash (which still had no publisher), your work had staggered to a halt, you were stuck and confused, you had not written a poem in more than a year, and you were slowly coming to the realization that you would never be able to write again. Such was the spot you were in that winter evening more than thirty-two years ago when you walked into the high school gym to watch the open rehearsal of Nina W.'s work in progress. You knew nothing about dance, still know nothing about dance, but you have always responded to it with a soaring inner happiness whenever you see it done well, and as you took your seat next to David, you had no idea what to expect, since at that point Nina W.'s work was unknown to you. She stood on the gym floor and explained to the tiny audience that the rehearsal would be divided into two alternating parts: demonstrations of the principal movements of the piece by the dancers and verbal commentary from her. Then she stepped aside, and the dancers began to move around the floor. The first thing that struck you was that there was no musical accompaniment. The possibility had never occurred to you—dancing to silence rather than to music—for music had always seemed essential to dance, inseparable from dance, not only because it sets the rhythm and speed of the performance but because it establishes an emotional tone for the spectator, giving a narrative coherence to what would otherwise be entirely abstract, but in this case the dancers' bodies were responsible for establishing the rhythm and tone of the piece, and once you began to settle into it, you found the absence of music wholly invigorating, since the dancers were hearing the music in their heads, the rhythms in their heads, hearing what could not be heard, and because these eight young people were good dancers, in fact excellent dancers, it wasn't long before you began to hear those rhythms in your head as well. No sounds, then, except the sounds of bare feet thumping against the wooden floor of the gym. You can't remember the details of their movements, but in your mind you see jumping and spinning, falling and sliding, arms waving and arms dropping to the floor, legs kicking out and running forward, bodies touching and then not touching, and you were impressed by the grace and athleticism of the dancers, the mere sight of their bodies in motion seemed to be carrying you to some unexplored place within yourself, and little by little you felt something lift inside you, felt joy rising through your body and up into your head, a physical joy that was also of the mind, a mounting joy that spread and continued to spread through every part of you. Then, after six or seven minutes, the dancers stopped. Nina W. stepped forward to explain to the audience what they had just witnessed, and the more she talked, the more earnestly and passionately she tried to articulate the movements and patterns of the dance, the less you understood what she was saying. It wasn't because she was using technical terms that were unfamiliar to you, it was the more fundamental fact that her words were utterly useless, inadequate to the task of describing the wordless performance you had just seen, for no words could convey the fullness and brute physicality of what the dancers had done. Then she stepped aside, and the dancers began to move again, immediately filling you with the same joy you had felt before they'd stopped. Five or six minutes later, they stopped again, and once more Nina W. came forward to speak, again failing to capture a hundredth part of the beauty you had just seen, and back and forth it went for the next hour, the dancers taking turns with the choreographer, bodies in motion followed by words, beauty followed by meaningless noise, joy followed by boredom, and at a certain point something began to open up inside you, you found yourself falling through the rift between world and word, the chasm that divides human life from our capacity to understand or express the truth of human life, and for reasons that still confound you, this sudden fall through the empty, unbounded air filled you with a sensation of freedom and happiness, and by the time the performance was over, you were no longer blocked, no longer burdened by the doubts that had been weighing down on you for the past year. You returned to your house in Dutchess County, to the downstairs workroom where you had been sleeping since the end of your marriage, and the next day you began to write, for three weeks you worked on a text of no definable genre, neither a poem nor a prose narrative, attempting to describe what you had seen and felt as you'd watched the dancers dance and the choreographer talk in that high school gym in Manhattan, writing many pages to begin with and then boiling them down to eight pages, the first work of your second incarnation as a writer, the bridge to everything you have written in the years since then, and you remember finishing during a snowstorm late one Saturday night, two o'clock in the morning, the only person awake in the silent house, and the terrible thing about that night, the thing that continues to haunt you, is that just as you were finishing your piece, which you eventually called *White Spaces*, your father was dying in the arms of his girlfriend. The ghoulish trigonometry of fate. Just as you were coming back to life, your father's life was coming to an end.

In order to do what you do, you need to walk. Walking is what brings the words to you, what allows you to hear the rhythms of the words as you write them in your head. One foot forward, and then the other foot forward, the double drumbeat of your heart. Two eyes, two ears, two arms, two legs, two feet. This, and then that. That, and then this. Writing begins in the body, it is the music of the body, and even if the words have meaning, can sometimes have meaning, the music of the words is where the meanings begin. You sit at your desk in order to write down the words, but in your head you are still walking, always walking, and what you hear is the rhythm of your heart, the beating of your heart. Mandelstam: "I wonder how many pairs of sandals Dante wore out while working on the *Commedia.*" Writing as a lesser form of dance.

Cataloguing your travels ninety pages ago, you forgot to mention your journeys between Brooklyn and Manhattan, thirty-one years of traveling within your own city since your removal to Kings County in 1980, on average two or three times a week, which would add up to several thousand trips, many of them underground by subway, but many others back and forth across the Brooklyn Bridge in cars and taxis, a thousand crossings, two thousand crossings, five thousand crossings, it is impossible to know how many, but surely it is the trip you have taken more often than any other in your life, and not once have you failed to admire the architecture of the bridge, the curious but altogether satisfying blend of old and new that distinguishes this bridge from all others, the thick stone of the medieval Gothic arches at odds with and yet in harmony with the delicate spider webs of steel cables, once the tallest man-made structure in North America, and back in the days before the suicidal murderers visited New York, it was always the crossing from Brooklyn to Manhattan that you preferred, the anticipation of reaching the exact point where you could simultaneously see the Statue of Liberty in the harbor to your left and the downtown skyline looming in front of you, the immense buildings that would suddenly jump into sight, among them the Towers, of course, the unbeautiful Towers that gradually became a familiar part of the landscape, and even though you still marvel at the skyline whenever you approach Manhattan, now that the Towers are gone you can no longer make the crossing without thinking about the dead, about seeing the Towers burn from your daughter's bedroom window on the top floor of your house, about the smoke and ashes that fell onto the streets of your neighborhood for three days following the attack, and the bitter, unbreathable stench that forced you to shut all the windows of your house until the winds finally shifted away from Brooklyn on Friday, and even though you have continued to cross the bridge two or three times a week in the nine and a half years since then, the journey is no longer the same, the dead are still there, and the Towers are there as well—pulsating in memory, still present as an empty hole in the sky.

You heard the dead calling out to you—but only once, once in all the years you have been alive. You are not someone who sees things that are not there, and while you have often been confused by what you are seeing, you are not prone to hallucinations or fantastical alterations of reality. The same with your ears. Every now and then, while out on one of your walks through the city, you think you hear someone calling to you, think you hear the voice of your wife or daughter or son shouting your name from across the street, but when you turn around to look for them, it is always someone else saying *Paul* or *Dad* or *Daddy*. Twenty years ago, however, perhaps twenty-five years ago, under circumstances far removed from the flow of your daily life, you experienced an auditory hallucination that continues to bewilder you with its vividness and power, the sheer volume of the voices you heard, even though the chorus of the dead screamed out in you for no more than five or ten seconds. You were in Germany, spending the weekend in Hamburg, and on Sunday morning your friend Michael Naumann, who was also your German publisher, suggested that the two of you pay a visit to Bergen-Belsen—or, rather, to the site where Bergen-Belsen had once stood. You wanted to go, even if a part of you was reluctant to go, and you remember the drive there on the nearly empty autobahn that overcast Sunday morning, a white-gray sky hanging over mile after mile of flat land, seeing a car that had crashed into a tree by the side of the road and the corpse of the driver lying on the grass, a body so inert and twisted that you immediately knew the man was dead, and there you were, sitting in the car and thinking about Anne Frank and her sister, Margot, who had both died in Bergen-Belsen, along with tens of thousands of others, the many thousands of others who perished there from typhus and starvation, random beatings, murder. The dozens of films and newsreels you had seen of the death camps were spooling through your head as you sat in the passenger seat of the car, and as you and Michael approached your destination, you found yourself growing more and more anxious and withdrawn. Nothing was left of the camp itself. The buildings had been torn down, the barracks had been demolished and carted away, the barbed-wire fences had vanished, and what stood there now was a small museum, a one-story structure filled with poster-sized black-and-white photographs along with explanatory texts, a grim place, an awful place, but so denuded and antiseptic that you found it hard to imagine the reality of the place as it had been during the war. You couldn't feel the presence of the dead, the horror of so many thousands crammed into that nightmare village surrounded by barbed wire, and as you walked through the museum with Michael (in your memory, you were the only people there), you wished the camp had been left intact so the world could have seen what the architecture of barbarism had looked like. Then you went outside, onto the grounds where the death camp had stood, but it was a grassy field now, a domain of lovely, well-tended grass stretching for several hundred yards in all directions, and if not for the various markers planted in the ground that indicated where the barracks had once been, where certain buildings had once been, there would have been no way to guess what had gone on there several decades earlier. Then you came to a patch of grass that was slightly elevated, three or four inches higher than the rest of the field, a perfect rectangle that measured about twenty feet by thirty feet, the size of a large room, and in one corner there was a marker in the ground that read: *Here lie the bodies of 50,000 Russian soldiers.* You were standing on top of the grave of fifty thousand men. It didn't seem possible that so many dead bodies could fit into such a small space, and when you tried to imagine those bodies beneath you, the tangled corpses of fifty thousand young men packed into what must have been the deepest of deep holes, you began to grow dizzy at the thought of so much death, so much death concentrated in such a small patch of ground, and a moment later you heard the screams, a tremendous surge of voices rose up from the ground beneath you, and you heard the bones of the dead howl in anguish, howl in pain, howl in a roaring cascade of full-throated, ear-splitting torment. *The earth was screaming.* For five or ten seconds you heard them, and then they went silent.

Talking to your father in your dreams. For many years now, he has been visiting you in a dark room on the other side of consciousness, sitting down at a table with you for long, unhurried conversations, calm and circumspect, always treating you with kindness and goodwill, always listening carefully to what you say to him, but once the dream is over and you wake up, you can't recall a single word either one of you said.

Sneezing and laughing, yawning and crying, burping and coughing, scratching your ears, rubbing your eyes, blowing your nose, clearing your throat, chewing your lips, rolling your tongue over the backs of your lower teeth, shuddering, farting, hiccuping, wiping sweat from your forehead, running your hands through your hair—how many times have you done those things? How many stubbed toes, smashed fingers, and knocks on the head? How many stumbles, slips, and falls? How many blinks of your eyes? How many steps taken? How many hours spent with a pen in your hand? How many kisses given and received?

Holding your infant children in your arms.

Holding your wife in your arms.

Your bare feet on the cold floor as you climb out of bed and walk to the window. You are sixty-four years old. Outside, the air is gray, almost white, with no sun visible. You ask yourself: How many mornings are left?

A door has closed. Another door has opened.

You have entered the winter of your life.

(2011)